THE SCALE OF PERFECTION

THE SCALE
OF PERFECTION

by Walter Hilton

Abridged and presented by
Illtyd Trethowan
Monk of Downside

ABBEY PRESS • ST. MEINRAD, IN 47577 • 1975

First published in U.S.A. by Abbey Press, 1975.

First published in the United Kingdom by Geoffrey Chapman,
a division of Cassell and Collier Macmillan Publishers Ltd.

The text is from *The Ladder of Perfection*, Penguin (1957),
translation by Leo Sherley-Price.

Copyright © text and commentary, Geoffrey Chapman Publishers, 1975.

Library of Congress Catalog Card Number: 75-19926
ISBN: 0-87029-055-X

Printed in the U.S.A.

CONTENTS

I Introduction

II The Text

Book One

(*NB The chapter numbers referred to are those of this edition. Numbers in
brackets refer to the original chapter numbers.*)

Contents

Book Two

I INTRODUCTION

I ——————————— Explaining the present book

The reason for making this abridgment of *The Scale of Perfection* is that it could be of great practical value not only for Christians but for anyone. Many have had to ask themselves in recent years whether they can go on holding their beliefs; many are beginning to ask themselves whether they can go on disbelieving in religion altogether. Fewer people go to church; but for more and more people the question of religion becomes an urgent personal one. If you think, as I do, that this ultimate question is not one which can be settled, in the end, by argument, but only by some sort of direct acquaintance with God, then it becomes a question of how one may be able to get in touch with him. And that is what prayer is about. But in the first instance we need encouragement if we are to attempt something which is thought to be very difficult, and then we want advice on how to set about it.

But surely it is absurd to apply to a famous medieval mystic? Won't it be discouraging to find ourselves so far from these heights, that is, supposing that the whole business isn't an illusion? Or, if we think that we see what he is driving at, may we not, in our inexperienced condition, fatally misunderstand it? I must explain what I meant by 'encouragement': Hilton can encourage us to believe that this business is *not* an illusion. We cannot expect to settle this question just by reading him (although that *could* be the occasion for seeing the truth which we are seeking), but we may be sufficiently impressed by him to decide that it is worthwhile facing the question in a businesslike way, if indeed there is one. And Hilton offers us what may prove to be one. Certain conditions must be fulfilled, he tells us, before we can hope to be aware of God's presence—the basic one, put into modern terms, is that we should want the truth above everything, be prepared to put up with everything for truth's sake. (On that one condition, I would urge, one can profitably use the agnostic's prayer: 'God, if there is a God, help me to realize that you are here'.) And we are most unlikely, if we follow Hilton's guidance, to suppose that we are running in the mystic way when we have not yet learned to walk in it.

William James has written somewhere that people who would not dream of regarding themselves as mystics can nevertheless have an inkling of what mystical writers are talking about, and this remark is often quoted to suggest that mystical writing can be far from discouraging to the enquirer. Bergson was led to see the truth of Christianity by reading the mystics. That was in the thirties, when Christian mysticism was, in some circles, 'in'. Recently, in the English-speaking world, it has had a very bad press. But interest in it has revived, partly because 'mysticism' (in a vague sense) is now 'in'.

That sense of the word makes it refer to a congeries of experiences ranging from those of mystics claiming to be in touch with God to those of drug-takers, with a general emphasis on a feeling of being 'one with Nature'. The idea is that all these experiences are, fundamentally, the same, and it may then seem that religious people interpret them in terms of their own illusions. From my point of view, it can be disastrously confusing to use the same word about states of consciousness which share only quite superficial characteristics and have a quite different origin. Christian theologians regard mysticism as a developed awareness of God in Christ. It does not follow, however, that this awareness is to be found only among professing Christians, although it follows from Christian principles of thought that it comes to men through the power which Christ won for us, the new life which his resurrection has made available for us, whether or not one realizes that this is in fact the case. So an interest in 'mysticism' (in the vague sense) is not something merely to be deplored by Christians. Behind the confusions there may prove to be something lurking which should be brought to light. And when this sort of vague interest leads people to take notice of Christian mysticism, Hilton's account, I venture to think, is likely to be more profitable to them than that of any other English mystic. My reasons for thinking so must be left for later on.

Yet *The Scale* is, at the time of writing, out of print and has been for some years, except for those chapters printed in Professor Eric Colledge's anthology, *The Medieval Mystics of England*. There is no immediate prospect of a reprinting, but it is hoped that Dom Gerard Sitwell's version will eventually reappear (it was published in 1953 by Burns Oates in their Orchard Series). Mr Leo Sherley-Price's version, published in 1957 (by Penguin Books) as *The Ladder of Perfection*, has been adopted for the present abridgment.

But why, it will be asked, an abridgment? Why not make the whole thing available like the translators just mentioned? To answer that I must explain that *The Scale* consists of two distinct books, which overlap to a considerable extent. The first was written, ostensibly at least, for the special needs of an anchoress, and a good deal of it, therefore, is of limited interest. The second, which is somewhat longer, was written (perhaps much later) at the instance of some person unknown but obviously with a public in view. The substance of that book is printed here; I have excluded only some introductory matter (amounting to about a tenth of it), a few sentences of no importance in later chapters and a short disquisition on angels near the end: some outstanding chapters from the earlier book are printed first (Professor Colledge prints an abridgment of that book but only chapters 21 to 25 of the second one). Christians in the past have been helped by many passages (in both books of *The Scale*) to persevere in prayer; these, I trust, are all present. Further reasons for excluding certain passages will emerge in the next section.

2 ━━━━━━━━━━━━━━━━ Hilton's points of view

In an earlier age spiritual writers regularly assumed that those who lived licentious lives were sinning against the light. Such people might scoff at religion in word, but they had been, of course, baptized, and they could not honestly disbelieve in God or his Church. So one had to be tough with them, in the first instance, paint their sins in the most lurid colours, charge them with ingratitude and scare them into repentance. It must be allowed that this was often, in the first instance, highly effective. Today 'hell-fire sermons' have become, at any rate, less usual. What now seems necessary, in the first instance, is to make people realize that God is love and that Christianity is the religion of love. It is indeed also necessary to insist that we are free to choose God or to reject him, so that the loss of him (however that may be envisaged) remains a possibility. But ranting at people seems less and less likely to produce good results, although some may still think that it ought to. It can be extremely off-putting for those who feel the attraction of the mystics and hope to gain enlightenment from them. To some extent Hilton shares the earlier point of view. (He never rants, however, although he sometimes refers to the pains of hell in a bland tone of voice which jars.) On the other hand, when he talks about love, he is extraordinarily persuasive. It seems necessary to examine his attitudes.

Hilton's writing, almost inevitably, reveals the presuppositions of his environment. He lapses occasionally into the language of a conventional anti-humanism, a sort of pessimism about human nature and the world in which we live. Perhaps more importantly, readers who do not accept the traditional Christian dogmas, even if they are willing to entertain them while reading him, may find that he sometimes refers to them in a rather disconcerting way. The fact is, I think, that there are two sides to Hilton. On one side, he is just a man of his time. His respect for authority goes beyond what we should regard as reasonable; he will take over contemporary attitudes of mind without question (it has been remarked that he denounces heretics with a severity even greater than that of some of his contemporaries). *In fine*, Hilton, on one side of him, is not a thinker. So in making the abridgment I have avoided, where possible, the obstacles which this can set up—plenty, however, still remain. But on his other side, Hilton is, in the word's literal sense, a *seer*, who thinks about what he sees and can help us to see it. That is his importance.

It may be useful to discuss these matters further. When he writes of the earlier stages of the spiritual ascent, Hilton seems sometimes just to follow the current conventions. He will speak of the redemption in terms of the Cross alone and as if Christ *bought* our freedom for us, in some literal sense, by his sufferings. He will speak of God as the watchful judge who will exact a terrible penalty for sin. He will make God's ways seem arbitrary, especially perhaps when he is speaking of the sacraments, although he certainly does not think of them as magic and knows that we must be rightly disposed if we are to benefit from them (he was in fact a very learned theologian, although—on the whole fortunately—he does not write like one). But when he begins to speak out of his own experience (when Book II of *The Scale* gets under way), the general atmosphere becomes different. God is the loving Father, who will do everything for us if only we allow him to act on us. It is the risen glorious Christ whom we meet in prayer and who unites us with himself. So it would seem that we rise from our sins in the power of his resurrection, the power of the new life which he came to bring; he has won it by passing through the gates of death to the victorious state in which his manhood is definitively empowered; we are empowered through our union with him. That is what modern theologians are claiming as the genuinely traditional and New Testament theology. So the redemption is no bargain with God. Those who look at it like this can feel at home again when Hilton becomes a first-hand witness.

It seems to me, then, that when he is gentle, encouraging and illuminating, we have the Hilton who matters (these are the qualities which have been always associated with him); when he seems harsh or blinkered, I suppose him to be talking at second hand. It is not that he is insincere but that he is just taking things for granted. Sometimes he will seem simple-minded; but he has to allow for the needs of simple-minded people.

Another warning may be needed. Hilton makes casual references to Christian beliefs which, taken in isolation, could at times mislead. He will speak of the three 'persons' of the Trinity in a way which may make them seem three Gods. What in fact he believes, as becomes quite clear, is the orthodox doctrine that God *is* three interdependent 'persons'. He will speak of 'the elect' and of God's 'especial grace' in a way which could suggest, though only at first glance, that he is making God responsible for everything, evil included (some pious talk about providence in the pulpit does really lead to such a conclusion). But Hilton's language can indeed strongly suggest that his teaching is of use only to certain people. Is this in fact the case? Something must now be said about this important question.

What Hilton is specially concerned with is, as Dom Gerard Sitwell puts it (in the Introduction to his version of *The Scale*), an awareness of the life of sanctifying grace; after speaking of the support in Catholic theology for this view of contemplation, Dom Gerard goes on to say: 'I do not think that any writer on the subject has drawn attention to it so clearly as Hilton has done.' Sanctifying grace is the new life which Christ offers us; faith is the entrance to it. Is the *awareness* of it possible only for some? We may suppose that we are not all called to the highest degree of it, star differing from star in glory, and that Hilton, writing about the heights of mysticism, may be speaking of God's 'especial grace' with that in mind. But Hilton is not much concerned in *The Scale* with degrees of perfection. It is the 'state of perfection' in general which he offers as a goal to his readers. And on closer inspection he proves never to say that anyone is *constitutionally* incapable of reaching it; if anyone is prepared to take the necessary steps, there is no reason to doubt that God will give it to him. The graces which he will receive are special graces, because in fact so few are fit to receive them.

Hilton divides people into 'actives' and 'contemplatives', but it does not follow that 'actives' cannot become 'contemplatives'. On the contrary, Hilton is anxious that they should. Why, then, is he so insistent, as most mystical writers are, that his pages should not fall into the hands of 'actives'? It seems to be because they might attempt contemplative prayer before they were properly prepared for it. But since the danger of this has been emphasized so much in their own writings, it will seem odd that the mystics should still be worried by it. The explanation, I suppose, is that there were so many people about who were only semi-literate.

So Hilton encourages us all to think that this awareness of grace is available for us. In a letter to some person in high position he urges him to keep the contemplative goal in view; aiming at it is not incompatible with the performance of his duties, however difficult it may become in practice. If circumstances prevent us from a full development on earth, we shall be ready for it in heaven if we do all we can. But now we have to face another point of view which may well seem very odd to us: Hilton thinks that, although the awareness of grace is most desirable for us, we can in fact make do without it. This results from his attitude to the question of religious *conviction*.

Making sense of faith was not, for Hilton, as it is for many of us, an urgent issue. He speaks of it as 'laid on', so to say, in baptism. God gives it to us in our infancy, and so long as we do not repudiate it or fall into serious sin we remain in the right way. We have the life of grace, and although we need not be aware of it God makes us certain, somehow, that we have it. The truth of Christianity was obvious for Hilton's society, and he felt no need, apparently, to think the matter out. But for us, who feel this need, his own teaching about the awareness of grace suggests an answer. For, as he makes very clear, this is an awareness of God in Christ. It is his presence in us of which we are aware. We can be convinced that God has spoken in Christ because we can be *aware* of him in Christ and in his Church. That is how conviction is formed in a Christian's mind. And he needs this conviction if he is to be an authentic Christian.

There are other accounts of faith's certainty in Christian theology.

This is not the place for discussing them, but it seems fair to say that they are coming more and more to appear insufficient and that the view which I have just mentioned has been gaining ground rapidly in recent years. It must be added that this awareness may be most obscure at first, registered perhaps only as an absolute demand upon one to accept Christ's teaching. But it must be based on a contact of the mind with God, a contact which may have needed to be strengthened before it could issue in conviction. If this is right, Hilton's teaching on prayer proves to have vital importance. The awareness to which it leads us must be available for everyone, for God gives his grace to everyone who does what he can about it. He has made contact with us already, Hilton will suggest to us, if we want the truth above all things. For a desire, he points out, implies an awareness of something.

Some Christians will say that faith is not a matter of certainty: it is based on trust in Christ. To put it baldly, we *bet* on the truth of Christianity; faith is based, intellectually, only on probable arguments. That is not the view of the New Testament writers, and so traditional theology has always held that faith is a gift over and above the gift of our reasoning powers. It does mean trust in Christ, but that must be based on some contact with God, however we may explain that contact (as I have indicated, there are various accounts of it; for a discussion of this question and of others raised in the present section I may be allowed to refer to my *Mysticism and Theology*).*

In fine, if mysticism is the development of faith (as so many theologians say), then faith must have something in common with it. Circumstances may prevent us from reaching that full development of it on which Hilton's interest is concentrated, but we must be ready to advance towards it as far as we can. Some will say that I ought not to speak of 'mysticism' at all until a certain special passivity in the life of prayer has been established, and the word is often used in that restricted sense. But we do need some word for faith's development, taken in its whole range, and I cannot think of any other. 'Mysticism', in ordinary, non-technical conversation, is taken to mean not knowledge *about* God but a knowledge, an experience, *of* him, and that is the present topic.

* (Geoffrey Chapman, 1975.)

3 ═══════════════════ A run-through of the text

There is not much need to interpret Hilton. He speaks plainly enough as a rule, and it is the method rather than the matter of his writing that may be at first a little bewildering. He does not take us up his ladder in an uninterrupted progress but will often bring us down again to lower rungs. A spiritual ascent, he tells us, is impossible if it is not at the same time a moral one, and so we are never allowed to forget that there is the danger of slipping back, losing our foothold through carelessness. This might lead gradually to a loss of interest in God and so to a general disintegration. But even when we are not ourselves to blame there may be times when we have to fall back on methods of prayer which were thought to have served their turn. Hilton keeps in mind the journey as a whole and its vicissitudes even when he is discussing its final stages, and when we realize this the untidiness of his account ceases, I think, to trouble us. The chapter-headings are a help, but it may be an advantage to have a rough map of the course in its first stages, indicating the movements back and forth. For purposes of the present section, little will need to be said about the rest of it.

So I shall now run through the contents of this earlier part, trying at the same time to bring out the usefulness, as I see it, of particular passages. The first of the passages here printed sums up a good deal of *The Scale*, and is typical of its general tone. We notice that for Hilton 'God' and 'Jesus Christ' are one, for the divine Word himself acts in Jesus Christ. Prayer, he tells us, is a 'real perception of God'. That is what we are all bound for, in the end. Hilton then warns us against attaching importance to physical sensations which may be occasioned by prayer—apparently because the writings of Richard Rolle had led to some misunderstanding. The theme of the passages which follow is that we should make room in our minds and hearts so that God may act upon them, for we are always at the receiving end in our relations with him. But (Book One, Chapter 4 (27)) we may not find this advice of much help for a start. Our interest may still be only feeble, and to keep it going we may need to use set prayers. For some today there can only be at first what I have referred to as the agnostic's prayer; but to be present at the Church's central prayer, the Eucharist, can lead to their finding themselves praying it.

When the desire of God has been really aroused (Chapter 5 (29)), we shall begin to realize that we have wasted a great deal of time and perhaps that we have made a great mess of things. God is becoming more real to us, and we want to get rid of our encumbrances. We ask for his help, not because he needs persuading to give it but because we put ourselves in the way of accepting it. Traditional formulas of petitionary prayer become meaningful (the second stage of prayer), and, almost imperceptibly perhaps, expressions of gratitude begin to mingle with them. Hilton describes (Chapter 6 (30)) the powerful effects which this sort of prayer can have. He is moving very fast because it proves that his anchoress needs help with the third stage (Chapter 7 (32)), that of wordless prayer. His advice on distractions (Chapter 8 (33)) is the usual advice, but it has an unusual force.

All that may seem very far away, but Hilton goes back (Chapter 10 (42)) to the indispensable condition for all advance. It is the rooting up of a 'false and misplaced love of self' (much of Book One is concerned with the disastrous consequences of such a love). This chapter and the next demand the closest attention if there is to be any profit in reading on. The extracts which follow return to the original theme with a warmth and simplicity, a natural eloquence, which is so marked a feature of Book Two. The passages taken from Book One may be regarded in fact as a sort of preliminary canter. But before leaving it I have thought fit to insert two remarkable chapters on the love of our fellow-men, for it is so often supposed that the life of prayer is a selfish one. Nothing could be further from the truth. But there have been aberrations; often there has been a tendency for Christians to concentrate on their relations with God to the disregard of their duties to other people. Recently this helped to produce a violent reaction against all prayer in silence and solitude, which in modern conditions happens to be specially needed. Hilton makes clear (Chapter 18 (70)) that we must love ourselves 'in God' as well as other people. It is indeed our primary duty, for no one can take over that responsibility from us. And unless we do it we cannot give others the help that they need most.

In Book Two the contemporary habit of allegorizing scriptural passages (sometimes in an inaccurate rendering) becomes increasingly noticeable. It can be irritating, but it can also be useful, because Hilton is sometimes led by it to bring out his own point more effectively. The first passages from Book Two are necessary to introduce Hilton's distinction between those who are 'reformed in faith' and those who are 'reformed in faith and feeling', that is, those who have a clear awareness of God's presence. Hilton's great themes prove to be the gradual emergence and development of this awareness and its magnificent effects. Chapters 22–24 (14–16), on those who are not reformed at all, show that Hilton is just as anxious here as in Book One to emphasize the dangers of sin. But there is no touch of that disquieting relish which has sometimes infected such sermonizings, and no sentimentality. And what this leads up to is that grace will be given if it is asked for and will 'drive away the darkness'. Mere struggling is no good—asking for grace is asking for a light which empowers. But full reformation requires a complete turning-away from 'spiritual sickness' and may take a very long time (Chapter 25 (17)). Hilton pauses to insist in three more Chapters that whole-hearted effort is needed. He points out that some may be held up by an undue attachment to particular pious practices. And once more he turns back to the imperative need for eradicating the vices. But now there is a growing feeling that we have been launched upon a runway, most marked in a passage about humility (Chapter 28 (20)), which consists in seeing that 'Jesus does everything'. At last, in the next chapter, there is the take-off with the simile of the pilgrimage to Jerusalem. It is justly famous, but there are still better things to come.

Up to this point (about a third of the way through the abridged text) a reader may have been wondering whether he will get to the end. Now he will find, I hope, that his hesitations vanish. When Hilton has once become airborne like this, although he soon returns to warning us about the dangers which lie in wait on the spiritual ascent, it should seem pretty plain that he will be speaking again before long of the light by which he himself now seems to be surrounded. And in fact a note of triumph tends more and more to predominate until *The Scale*, for the last third of this text, becomes an almost unchecked flow of spiritual joy, the more impressive because it is so well controlled. Hilton is obviously speaking from his own experience, yet his account of the effects which are wrought by this enlightenment has something of the impersonality peculiar to the great artist. In a sense he just goes on repeating himself for most of

Book Two. In principle his teaching has been already stated. What he does is to make us realize more and more the importance of it.

There are, however, a few passages in Book Two where Hilton may seem to be confused or inconsistent. If they throw us off course, it is only for the moment; the questions which they raise are side-issues for Hilton's present purposes. But these questions have their importance, greater or less, and I shall devote the rest of this section to them. Readers who have no particular interest in them may pass quickly on without loss.

The language which Hilton uses about the human faculties is somewhat vague, although it is unlikely to cause real difficulty. In Chapter 21 (13) he is content to mention sense-perception and the reason, which 'itself has two powers', a higher and a lower. The lower power has an organizing function and in exercising it must 'always watch, respect and follow the higher rational faculty'; the soul is thus 'enabled to see God and spiritual things'. Towards the end of Chapter 28 (20) it proves that 'reason' will not succeed of itself in showing us that all good comes to us from God. For this we require a 'spiritual perception of truth'. It becomes clear that this means an awareness of God which has reached a certain point of development. It is this awareness with which Hilton is concerned, and what he says about the 'higher reason' is of importance for him only in connection with it. In the last paragraph of Chapter 39 (31) he tells us that the soul is to be 'reformed by the perfect knowledge of God'. And he then tells us that in the early stages of development people think of God in an imaginative way rather than by using the reason—they make *pictures* of him. But at a later stage they use 'reason, strengthened and illuminized by the Holy Spirit'. In other words, 'spiritual perception' now takes over, and imagination 'has little place'. God is strictly unimaginable. So Hilton thinks of 'reason' as leading us to God but as unable of itself to put us in touch with him. All that really matters is that something, which we might call the 'mind', is to be in touch with him.

Hilton, however, has more to say about imagination, and this may be rather puzzling. In Chapter 38 (30), after speaking of the soul as a 'spiritual mirror in which you may see the likeness of God', he says, referring apparently to the early imaginative states, that many souls who keep this mirror clean 'enjoy great fervour'. Does he mean that by thinking of the soul as an image of God they are *imagining* him? I think not, because in the following paragraph, still with reference to fervour in the early stages, he speaks of knowing 'Jesus in his man-hood through the imagination'. So it seems rather that what is re-flected in the mirror is the moral perfection of Jesus. In these pas-sages Hilton's purpose is again to contrast the use of imagination and the use of reason in the life of the spirit. He goes on to say that 'imagi-nation is stimulated by grace' in these early stages, 'because the spiritual perceptions are awakened to contemplate our Lord's human nature'; but at a later stage the soul 'contemplates the Godhead united to manhood in Christ', and there the imagination can have only a secondary role. 'Spiritual perceptions' must be taken here in a broad sense if they are only an enhancement of an imaginative activity. Dom Gerard Sitwell, in his note at this point, considers that Hilton is speaking of the 'imaginative visions' to which later spiritual writers so often refer. In any case this is not of great interest for him; it is a pass-ing phenomenon. It belongs to what he here calls 'the second degree of love', when God is still thought of in an anthropomorphic way, whereas in the third degree 'grace moves the soul to contemplate God in man'.

To pause on the 'degrees of love' for a moment will throw some more light on 'reason'. The second and third degrees belong to those who are, partly or wholly, 'reformed in feeling'; so it is no surprise to find that the first degree 'is reached by faith alone, when no know-ledge of God is conveyed by grace through the imagination or under-standing'. Grace, that is to say, is not using the imagination or the reason ('understanding' is presumably just another word for it). But Hilton regards all these degrees of love as based on some knowledge. And a passage in Chapter 38 (30) indicates that, although *grace* is not providing any for the man who is 'reformed in faith alone', he has some knowledge because he 'believes what the Church teaches about God'—he does so because he knows that the Church teaches the truth. He has what Hilton here calls a 'blind knowledge': 'the blind man', he goes on, 'has no means of knowing that he is in sunlight, but believes it if a truthful person tells him so'. Hilton proceeds at once to call such a belief 'a degree of knowledge'. What he must mean is that the man cannot get to know the truth directly himself but only by knowing that the Church teaches the truth. And *that* he must know by reason alone for, according to Hilton, grace is not yet working through it.

I have suggested that faith as an awareness of grace may be regis-tered simply as an absolute obligation to accept the teaching of Christ (nowadays it is often held that the acceptance of an absolute obligation to one's fellow-men is an acceptance of the absolute value which is in fact God himself, although he may not be yet recognized). Thus even those Christians who seem altogether 'activist' may be in touch with God himself, although they do not realize this, in heeding the voice of conscience (in so far, at least, as it declares to them the law of charity). But they may well need to *concentrate* on this awareness of God if they are not to lose touch with him. I mention these considerations here because the next topic which seems to need discussion presents us with the same sort of situation.

Hilton writes in Chapter 49 (41): 'Do not be surprised when all consciousness of grace is sometimes withdrawn from one who loves God.' We must take him to mean all *consoling* consciousness of grace. For he has said in Chapter 32 (24) that the 'light' which the Lord brings us 'is sometimes full of pain, and sometimes pleasant and consoling'. It is clearly his general doctrine that the desire of God derives from an experience, however dim and unsatisfying, of his presence. So there too it is a matter of *recognizing* the true state of affairs.

Again in Chapter 49 (41), Hilton complicates things by attributing the (apparent) absence of God first to our 'natural weakness' and then to God's providential dealings with us. I may be allowed to make a proposal about that. God will turn our failures to good, if we let him; he does not plan them, but he enables us to profit by them. His attitude is one of constant generosity, but he does not override our moral freedom. That is why there is a 'problem of evil'. What he offers is always what is best for the whole situation to which men's failures have contributed so damagingly—and, if this is so, we cannot hope to perceive his designs in the occurrence of particular events.

There is no ground, I think, for attributing to Hilton the baffling doctrine of a wholly *unconscious* contemplation which some spiritual writers may seem to teach. But I ought to say that the one passage in *The Scale* which I find really obscure might be interpreted by some in such a sense. In Chapter 49 (41) Hilton speaks of a man who 'has entered the state of perfection' but 'does not recognize the presence of grace', so that 'he will not be grateful when it comes to him'. I do not know what he has in mind. In this chapter he allows himself to speak of 'the presence of grace' when he obviously means 'the awareness of grace'. The presence of grace apart from the awareness of it must be, for purposes of Hilton's present discussion, the state of soul in which we are fitted to have this awareness when the requisite conditions, mental, moral and physical, are all present. At the end of the chapter he tells us that he has been speaking of an awareness of 'special grace' as opposed to 'the ordinary grace possessed and experienced by a man through faith and goodwill towards God'. I have suggested that if he had concerned himself with the 'problem of faith' he might have found reason to think that all the faithful, properly so-called, have the awareness, in some measure, of the same grace. Here, it will be noted, he does allow that *something* is 'experienced' by all of them.

The passages discussed above should present no more than incidental difficulties to the reader who bears in mind Hilton's 'points of view' as described in the previous section. When he has once come to realize that Hilton's great theme is the spreading of God's light in our darkness he will take such things in his stride.

4 ═══════════════ On some notable passages

There are certain passages in Book Two which speak for themselves and need no gloss but which deserve special notice because they obviate difficulties presented by so many other writers on mysticism.

I shall take first what Hilton tells us about 'darkness' in Chapters 32 to 35 (24 to 27). The darkness of which he is now speaking is no longer just the darkness of sin. It is a darkness into which we are plunged when we turn away from 'worldly desires'. There is darkness because the false light of these desires has been extinguished and the true light has not yet replaced it. But it is the first glimmer of that light which has caused it. Since it is only a glimmer this state is predominantly one of darkness, but it becomes more and more a 'glowing darkness'. It is a time of waiting. It can be very painful, but it leads to a state of profound peace which is the 'gateway to contemplation'. Hilton speaks of it at the beginning of Chapter 35 (27) as 'a genuine phase of this darkness', because 'it consists firstly of self-knowledge, and then of self-transcendence through a burning desire to see Jesus; or more accurately, the experience is itself a spiritual perception of Jesus'. That sums up what Hilton says about darkness in *The Scale*, except for those passages in Chapter 49 (41) to which I referred above. In Chapter 33 (25) he has said: the soul 'is fully conscious of something beyond itself which as yet it neither knows nor possesses, but it has an ardent longing for it'. Plainly this means that it *is* in contact with something, although it may not realize what that is.

It seems to me that Hilton's account of this is more generally applicable and at least in one respect more intelligible than others which are better known. That of St John of the Cross, some two centuries later, is the most famous. It is more dramatic and much more alarming; it distinguishes a 'night of sense' from a 'night of spirit', and distinguishes 'active' and 'passive' phases in each. The 'night of spirit' is something to be expected at a *further* stage as a fresh development markedly different from the previous one (these may be fairly common phenomena in the West, but Eastern Christians are said, as a rule, to escape them). Hilton describes an unbroken development over which a single principle presides, that of disposing ourselves to receive God's gift of himself. And St John gives as one explanation of the darkness that one is 'blinded by excess of light', a difficult conception in the present context. Hilton's account does not present us with it. 'Excess of light' would be easier to understand of an initial bemusement, a transient condition at the beginning of the union to which the darkness is only a prelude (Hilton and St John agree that this union pours 'light' upon the mind).

The Cloud of Unknowing also speaks of 'excess of light' as a cause of the darkness, and regards this as the state of affairs in which the contemplative must expect to remain with only the possibility of an occasional gleam of light; yet, in what seems an inconsistent way, the unknown author of the book does speak of the 'cloud' at times as a source of peace and comfort, and Hilton is thought to be using him on this topic. In fact there are verbal similarities between *The Scale* and *The Cloud* in a number of places. But the two books differ fundamentally. The passage which I shall now quote from Book Two of *The Scale* (the opening of Chapter 42 (34)) is in direct contradiction of *The Cloud*.

But since the ultimate joy and end of the soul depends upon this knowledge of God, you may perhaps wonder why I said earlier that the soul should desire nothing but the love of God . . . love derives from knowledge, and not knowledge from love; consequently the happiness of the soul is said to derive chiefly from this knowledge and experience of God, to which is conjoined the love of God. And the better God is known the more he is loved. But inasmuch as the soul cannot attain this knowledge, or the love that derives from it, without God who is Love, I said that you should desire love alone.

For God's love alone guides the soul to this vision and knowledge. Hilton's earlier insistence on desiring love alone might be more naturally interpreted, perhaps, as an insistence on keeping one's attention on God and desiring to attend better. But that makes no difference to the firm teaching of these lines about knowledge and love, which have the great advantage of appealing to common sense. *The Cloud*, on the other hand, tells us that God 'may well be loved, but not thought' (Chapter 6). 'By love', the passage continues, 'he may be caught and held, but by thinking never'. This is intelligible in so far as it warns the contemplative against thinking *about* God in prayer, having *ideas* about him, thinking at second hand as opposed to experiencing. But *The Cloud* does not allow for any *experiencing* by the mind as a goal which may be expected. God may 'perhaps send out a shaft of spiritual light' on occasion (Chapter 29). But a constant theme of the book is summed up towards the end of it in the statement that one 'will always find that a cloud of unknowing is between him and God' (Chapter 69). There is 'something you are completely ignorant of stirring you to will and desire you know not what' (Chapter 34). And, still more plainly, God is said to be 'incomprehensible' to the 'knowing power' but 'all comprehensible' to the 'loving power' (Chapter 4). This is the baffling doctrine, so often found in such writings, that God is in direct contact with the will and the desires but not with the intelligence. St Thomas Aquinas teaches that we are united to God by love rather than by knowledge, and St John of the Cross follows him in this. Hilton rejects that doctrine in the passage just quoted.

Professor David Knowles in *The English Mystical Tradition* writes (p. 112): 'Like the author of *The Cloud*, Hilton preaches the primacy of love. . . .' He then refers to this same passage from *The Scale* and points out in a footnote that Hilton, in a minor work called *Bonum Est*, writes: 'Where knowing faileth, there love hitteth.' But that does not alter the fact that the passage from *The Scale* says something quite different. It is commonly accepted that Book Two of *The Scale* is the work of Hilton's maturity, and we may suppose that he had come to change his mind on the subject. Obviously love has the primacy in the sense that everything depends, in the practical order, on our doing our duty, fixing our attention upon God. But that is not the present question. Here we are asking what contemplation *is*—not what its necessary *condition* is, but what constitutes it. Professor Eric Colledge in *The Medieval Mystics of England* (p. 65), discussing the strange suggestion that Hilton in his young days was himself the author of *The Cloud*, remarks that *The Cloud* teaches a 'non-cognitive union' whereas *The Scale* teaches a cognitive one. Dame Helen Gardner had noted in 1937 Hilton's 'insistence on the element of cognition in the highest mystical states' ('Walter Hilton and the Mystical Tradition in England', *Essays and Studies* by members of the English Association, vol. XXII, p. 19). So the passage in *The Scale* which we have been considering is, in the judgment of these two scholars, no passing aberration but Hilton's considered teaching.

I have been taking it that *The Cloud* is concerned with a darkness which for Hilton and St John is only a preliminary to a union which both of them refer to in terms of light. As Professor Knowles puts it, '. . . whereas for the author of *The Cloud* the contemplative stands as it were between a cloud of forgetting (of creatures) and a cloud of unknowing (of God), the soul in *The Scale* enters into a night . . . and emerges therefrom into the light of God' (*op. cit.*, pp. 69–70). But it has been held that *The Cloud* means by 'darkness' both the realization that God is incomprehensible in the sense that our knowledge is never exhaustive of him, and an awareness of him which is so different from knowledge of any other sort that it can be referred to only paradoxically as 'ignorance'. In that case *The Cloud* would be speaking paradoxically of the union to which Hilton and St John refer in more straightforward terms. There is a long and very influential tradition in which language is used in just that way. It can be misunderstood, and it is a great advantage in *The Scale* that it is not open to this misunderstanding.

The tradition to which I have just referred is commonly called the 'Dionysian' one since it goes back to a writer (of the fifth century, it seems) who styled himself 'Dionysius the Areopagite'. It may have reached some English mystics by way of German and Flemish writers (Eckhart, Suso, Tauler and Ruysbroeck). And it uses *negative* language about union with God ('effacement' and even 'unconsciousness' as well as 'darkness'). Joseph Maréchal observed some fifty years ago in his great work entitled (in the English translation) *Studies in the Psychology of the Mystics*: 'It would be childish of us to allow ourselves to be imposed upon by these expressions which have their [affirmative] counterpart beside them' (p. 193). And here we have to face the fact that some writers interpret this tradition in a peculiarly disastrous way. They describe the soul as 'blinded by excess of light' in the union itself. We can see a meaning for that here; when there is an outpouring of light, not just a glimmer, it can blind the eyes, and we could take this language to refer paradoxically to the ineffable character of the divine illumination. But such writers, in particular many Eastern Christians in our own day, sometimes insist that we must take this 'blindness' to mean a total unintelligibility. The union, they say, surpasses and indeed contradicts our human intelligence. It is a union of love, not of knowledge. The importance of Hilton's rejection of that doctrine may now be even more apparent.

It is, to put it mildly, discouraging to be told that union with God has nothing to do with awareness in any normal sense of the word. And then when the mystics say that it does not really matter whether or not there is any 'experience' of God, one might be led to suppose that they regard union with him as a state of affairs of which one can be wholly unconscious. What they are driving at, as a rule, is that there can be contact with God even when one's *feelings* are predominantly disagreeable ones. Hilton says (as we have seen) that the initial contacts are compatible with much darkness; he also says that when we are fit for union itself we may be prevented from experiencing it by a variety of contingent circumstances. The notable passage which I shall now quote from Chapter 49 (41) sums up his view on the present subject:

> But you might say that we should love by faith alone, and have no desire for spiritual experiences nor overestimate them if they occur.... I reply that we should not desire physical experiences.... We should desire always to be conscious—so far as we may—of the lively inspiration of grace brought about by the spiritual presence of God within our souls. We should desire to contemplate him constantly with reverence, and always to feel the sweetness of his love in the wondrous nearness of his presence. This should be our life, and this our experience of grace, for God is the source of all grace, and grants this gift as he wills, to some in greater measure and to others less. ... And this experience is the goal towards which we should direct our lives and exertions. ...

That is pretty plain. It will be noticed that, according to Hilton, although union with God, light unmixed with darkness, is everyone's goal, there are degrees of this union to which some are called and not others.

In the next chapter Hilton makes sure that we do not misunderstand what he has been saying about an 'experience of grace':

> . . . the eyes of the soul turn to God and contemplate him clearly, and it knows with certainty that it knows and sees him. I do not mean that it sees him as he is in the fullness of his Godhead, but that it sees him to whatever extent he wills to reveal himself to a pure soul in this mortal life, according to the measure of its purity. For you can be sure that every experience of grace is an experience of God himself. . . . You may possibly wonder why I say at one time that grace does all this, and at another that it is divine love, or Jesus, or God. My reply is that when I say that grace does it I mean both divine love, Jesus, and God, for all are one and inseparable.

The passage is especially notable because there has been an unwillingness on the part of some theologians to allow that the mind can ever be in *direct* contact with God in this present life on the ground that this is reserved for the next. Nobody today is likely to question Hilton's orthodoxy in the matter. If we have knowledge of God at all, I should argue, it must have a character of directness. It may seem strange to some that such knowledge can be nevertheless a limited one. One can only reply that it is experienced as such.

But the knowledge of which Hilton speaks is a knowledge of *God in Christ* (this is not the language of *The Cloud*). Chapter 40 (32) begins with the assurance that, when the soul is purified, 'our Lord Jesus in his goodness and mercy . . . opens the eyes of the soul to see and know him, bathing it in his own blessed light. . . .' Hilton goes on to say that, although the soul's knowledge is limited and always will be, even in heaven, it recognizes him as 'changeless being, as sovereign power, sovereign truth and sovereign goodness. . . .' The soul 'venerates God in man'. And 'even were no other living person to believe in Jesus or love him, its own faith and love would never lessen, for its own certainty is so absolute that it cannot help but believe'. This is not the way in which hallucinated persons might be expected to talk. Hilton has stated the doctrine of the incarnation in Chapter 38 (30): 'I do not say that we should separate the divine nature of Christ from the human, but that we should love Jesus both as God and man, for in him God is united to man, and man to God. . . .' So he would have no use for the talk which we hear nowadays, in most unexpected quarters, about a change in God when God is united to man. If dogma is the crystallization of the faithful's experience, the mystics speak to us in these matters with a special authority. At a time when the central doctrines of Christianity are being questioned by so many who used to maintain them, Hilton's words at the end of Chapter 40 (32) are peculiarly relevant: 'For a soul that has experienced a little of this union with Jesus, I think that nothing remains but to abandon and ignore everything else, and devote itself entirely to obtaining a clearer knowledge and a deeper love of Jesus, and in him of all the Blessed Trinity.' And again in Chapter 54 (46) he tells us: 'The soul then begins to perceive a little of the mysteries of the Blessed Trinity.'

It will be remembered that in Chapter 42 (34) Hilton emphasizes that it is God's love for us which makes knowledge of him possible. Towards the end of the chapter he enunciates what I venture to call a fundamental principle for any viable Christian metaphysics:

> We ourselves do nothing more than allow him to act as he wills, for the most that we can do is to yield ourselves readily to the working of his grace. Yet even that readiness does not originate in us, but in him, so that all good that we do is due to him, although we do not realize this.

(Hilton then goes on to say that God 'does even more'; for 'he opens the eyes of the soul in a wonderful way, shows it the vision of God...'.) Professor Knowles quotes this passage and observes that it states, 'even more accurately than *The Cloud*, the distinction between what theologians know as "operant" and "co-operant" grace' (*op. cit.*, p. 112). It seems to me that these scholastic formulas blur rather than bring out the profound truth to which Hilton is pointing in the language of experience and with a most appropriate simplicity. The good that we do is God's gift to us. But we are not puppets in his hands. For we have the mysterious power to *refuse* his gift. We can perhaps see dimly that, if we are to be *united* with him, it could not be otherwise. This is another state of affairs which may be disconcerting for abstractive thought but is surely a fact of experience.

There is also a distinction accepted by some theologians between 'infused' and 'acquired' contemplation interpreted by them in various ways. In Chapter 43 (35) Hilton describes a state of affairs which might seem to justify it. Some people, he says, 'produce the feeling of love' by 'external discipline' and 'obedience to reason'. And sometimes 'God transforms this natural aspiration . . . into spiritual affection'. Hilton then points out that even the 'natural affections' cannot be produced without grace. But 'in those whose love of God is imperfect his love works indirectly through the natural affections; but in those whose love is perfect God works directly, implanting his own spiritual affections. . . .'. I take him to mean that the former are sometimes raised to contemplation on the occasion of a 'natural' and remote preparation for it, whereas the latter prepare themselves simply by waiting upon God (as he puts it, they 'allow the Holy Spirit to guide them'). The former, however, might be thought to 'acquire' contemplation in the sense that their efforts on the 'natural' plane remain the basis of it or rather a sort of material which it informs. But it is clear that this would be inconsistent with Hilton's position. What he is really concerned with throughout this chapter is that there is all the difference between love of God based on an obscure faith and the workings of reason, on the one hand, and a love based on a genuine *awareness* of God's presence and activity on the other. Contemplation for him is this loving awareness which is always 'infused' in the sense that it is God's special gift to those who are fit for it. We could also say that it is always 'acquired' in the sense that it must be prepared for—and the appropriate way to prepare for it, Hilton is saying, is just to put oneself at God's disposal, not to obstruct his activity. That is what he calls the 'spiritual' way.

So Chapter 43 (35) proves to make the same point as the previous one. It is also relevant to another tricky distinction, that between 'active' and 'passive' states of prayer:

> The more fully that grace enables the soul to recognize its own nothingness in the light of God's truth—sometimes without any outward signs of fervour—and the less it is conscious of loving and knowing God, the nearer it approaches to perceiving the gift of God's love. For it is then under the control of love, which directs the soul, causing it to forget itself and be conscious only that God is working within it. The soul is then more passive than active. . . .

Some people talk of 'purely passive' prayer. The 'perceiving' of which Hilton here speaks is clearly both passive and active, like all knowledge—but in the highest degree because this is what knowledge is *for*. It unites us, like all knowledge, with what is not ourselves and makes us live in it, but without merging us with it so that we cease to be ourselves. Some people talk of a complete disappearance of self-consciousness in prayer. *The Cloud*, for instance, uses such language in a well-known passage. It seems to me that it can mean only the disappearance of self-consciousness in the sense that the feeling of *apartness* disappears. In principle the mind is 'absorbed' in God in the same sort of way as it is when one is, say, listening to a Brandenburg Concerto. That must be what Hilton means by saying that 'the less it is conscious of loving and knowing God, the nearer it approaches to perceiving the gift of God's love'. It is concerned not with its own activity but with God. And here it becomes difficult to distinguish between knowing and loving. They seem to be two sides of a coin, and we can call this either a passive activity or an active passivity, as we will.

Finally, there is a sentence in Chapter 48 (40) which is highly significant. Hilton has been talking about renouncing 'worldly love of creatures', which the soul, he says, can 'easily forgo', for it is 'so deeply conscious of the intimate and blessed presence of God'. He goes on: 'I do not say that it will not longer love or think of other creatures, but rather that it will think of them at the right times, and will regard and love them with a free and spiritual love, not with an anxious and carnal love as heretofore.' This is the love of creatures 'in God', described so wonderfully by St John of the Cross in his *Spiritual Canticle*. So Hilton, in the end, is not anti-humanist. He uses 'free' here (to be precise, the manuscripts, so I understand, read 'ghostly and freely, not fleshly and painfully' at this point) in a way in which we can no longer use it in English. Here the context makes the meaning plain. It is still common enough in seventeenth-century poetry (in *King Lear*, for instance, Edgar says to his father: 'Bear free and patient thoughts'). It is the measure of what we have lost. Hilton can help us to regain it partly because he is so obviously an Englishman.

5 ══════════════ Hilton's life and works

Here I shall simply list the findings of scholars so far as they seem of sufficiently general interest. Since the only evidence for the facts of Hilton's life comes from manuscripts which are often unreliable and make conflicting statements, there is very little that can be positively asserted about it. No one now questions that he became a Canon of the Augustinian Priory of Thurgarton, near Southwell in Nottinghamshire, in about 1385 or that he died there about 1395. In some of his Latin writings he describes himself as living the life of a hermit; it would appear that he found himself unsuited to it and found happiness in the regular religious life (since he was steeped in a theological tradition which goes back through the Victorians to Augustine—and therefore to St Paul and the Fourth Gospel—it was natural that he should feel at home with the Austin Canons). The appearance of his name in certain documents leads to the conclusion that he had studied at Cambridge. Otherwise all that can be said, on the evidence of his letters and other works, is that he was a well-known spiritual director.

But we have to see this apparently uneventful life in its historical context. Hilton was writing during the Great Schism and in the middle of the Hundred Years' War. He cannot have been unaffected by the Peasants' Revolt in 1381, when Wat Tyler captured London. In 1388 the Prior of Thurgarton was appointed to deal with the local Lollards, who seemed to be carrying all before them. At the same time the Austin Canons were closely concerned with the struggle against the Wycliffite heresy. There are signs that they had troubles of their own. Certainly in the earlier part of the century there had been some laxity among them. The Priory was an important one, involved in much business, exposed to the dangers which that always brings to the life of such a community. All this gives a special significance to the 'serene homeliness' which Dr Gardner found in the article already quoted, as the peculiar mark of Hilton's writing (his serenity may seem even more remarkable to us, some forty years on, than it did when her article was written).

If Hilton had not written *The Scale*, he would not count as a writer of the first rank. Nevertheless other works of his contain much of great value. In 1910 *Of Angels' Song* was published in *The Cell of Self-Knowledge*, Edmund Gardner's edition of the seven mystical treatises by various hands printed by Henry Pepwell in 1521; in ten short pages we find the teachings of *The Scale* in words of exquisite beauty, and in particular it enlarges on 'the freedom . . . that a man hath over all creatures, the which dignity he may so recover by grace here, that every creature savour to him as it is'. In 1929 Miss Dorothy Jones produced *Minor Works of Walter Hilton* (in the Orchard Series of Burns Oates and Washbourne), which contains five treatises. I have had occasion above to mention two of them: a letter to a man in high

position, known as *Mixed Life*, which develops into a glowing account
of contemplative prayer, and *Bonum Est* on Psalm 91, which, as we
have seen, teaches the doctrine of *The Cloud* about the 'faiiing' of
knowledge (here it may be remarked that, although Miss Jones regards this treatise as Hilton's, she does not claim to have proved it
beyond question). The other three pieces are a translation of a work
described in most manuscripts as 'found in Master Lewis de Fonti-
bus' book at Cambridge' known as *Eight Chapters on Perfection*, and
meditations on Psalm 90 and the Canticle of Zachary, *Qui Habitat* and
Benedictus. Miss Jones remarks that in the latter part of *Qui Habitat*
'the writer attains a degree of sublimity equal to the work of Hilton in
the latter part of Book Two of *The Scale of Perfection*'; she draws
attention in detail to the close resemblances between them. And she
points out that '*Benedictus* also bears the stamp of Hilton'. It is most
desirable that at least these two treatises, together with *Mixed Life* and
Of Angels' Song, should become more readily accessible. Some of
Hilton's writings still remain in manuscript, and there are probably
others which have not yet been discovered.

There is much more to be said about *The Goad of Love*, the translation, attributed with virtual certainty to Hilton, of the composite
work *Stimulus Amoris*, edited from manuscripts by Miss Clare Kirchberger and published in 1953. The substance of this work is an account of the spiritual life by a thirteenth-century Franciscan, James
of Milan—the rest of it is by unknown writers. Hilton treated it all
very freely, leaving some things out and adding a good deal in a way
which is extremely revealing. Miss Kirchberger has discussed this in
a long and most valuable Introduction. It would be impertinent in me
to praise the skill which she brought to her editorial task, since I do
not work in this field of scholarship. But I must express my gratitude
for the light which she has shed on the workings of Hilton's mind.
James of Milan, she points out, describes rapture and ecstasy in the
'language of a purely affective devotion', whereas Hilton 'in the forth-
rightness of his disposition' disliked these extravagances and cut them
out. Miss Kirchberger adds: 'His own experience led him to the conclusion that, however simplified and absorbing the contemplation of
the Blessed Trinity becomes, it is an experience not only of love but
also of knowledge.' For Hilton the theologian, she writes, 'the incarnation must be, as always, the complete and final mode of feeling and
expression'. And it is for this reason, and not just because of 'nascent
heresies' or current aberrations, that 'Hilton in his second version of

The Scale, throughout his translation of the *Stimulus*, occasionally in his other translations, enriched these works with so many additional references to the humanity of Jesus'. The fact that there was a revision of *The Scale* (actually only of Book One) has been the topic of much scholarly discussion. Miss Kirchberger has said here, I think, all that needs to be said about it for our present purposes.

Some of her other comments should be noticed. She points out that Hilton, so far from cutting down on the devotional meditations which precede and follow James of Milan's treatise, has sometimes amplified them; 'in the meditation on the *Ave Maria*, there are passages of such beauty of literary expression as to merit inclusion in any anthology of English medieval prose. In *The Scale* there are indications of his strong affective nature, but it is not developed with anything like the overflowing richness and variety' found in *The Goad of Love*, which 'offered an opportunity to Hilton the poet and lover, brings him into line with earlier English mystics and reveals to us something we should not have known . . .'. The reader of *The Scale* may find it of interest to have those remarks in mind. It is to be hoped that *The Goad of Love*, now out of print, may become available once more, perhaps in a condensed form.

We also learn that Hilton often softens the harshness of the original, avoids 'the self-centred turn' which its arguments so persistently take, omits the legal terms in which it refers to the Redemption, and, most importantly, rephrases talk about 'deification' with its suggestion that the soul becomes *merged* with God. We find here the same distinction between 'sensible' and 'spiritual' joys which we find in *The Scale*. (It appears that *The Goad of Love* was probably written shortly before the revision of Book One of *The Scale* and also before Book Two.) Hilton's additions to the original are by way of emphasizing 'the practice of the presence of God', 'the gathering together of the soul in all its faculties', and the importance of absolute reliance upon God's love. In the chapter about the Passion, when he is castigating sins of pride, 'there is a ring of genuine anguish in the self-depreciation, in the brutal choice of direct words for the camouflaged sins; there is the unmistakable echo of the unconditional surrender of the whole personality to God awaiting the reconciliation and unification of the soul, which suggests the famous passage in *The Scale*, Book Two, Chapter 43 (35)'. We find 'a miniature of Hilton the penitent, which will enhance our appreciation of the greater work'. Miss Kirchberger concludes with a tribute to his 'wonderful eye for imagery, simile and parable'. His work 'abounds in these sketches of things seen and remembered and used in the interpretation of spiritual truths'. The reader of *The Scale* will find plenty of them.

The mention of manuscripts and of Hilton's revision of Book One of *The Scale* may prompt the question whether we really know what he wrote. The answer is that at certain points we cannot be sure about his exact words, but it seems that there can be no question of our misunderstanding his thought in any way which really matters. Work began on a critical edition of *The Scale* a good many years ago, but there is still no immediate prospect of its appearing. Meanwhile there is (for the few who can get hold of it) Miss Evelyn Underhill's text, based on some of the manuscripts, in which the original Middle English readings are preserved but in modern spelling and with the substitution of modern words (about forty of them) for those which are now quite obsolete. This text was published in 1923. It is the first to be based on manuscript sources since the first printed edition of Wynkyn de Worde (1494), the edition chiefly used by translators before Miss Underhill's own became available. The version adopted in the present book (as also that of Dom Gerard Sitwell) is based on her text. Dom Gerard, who made use also of Wynkyn de Worde, tells us in his Introduction that there is 'practically complete agreement' between that text and hers 'except in the division of the chapters and the chapter headings'.

Originally I had hoped to print Miss Underhill's text, perhaps with a few further helps. In fact it is not at all difficult to read, even for those without experience of Middle English, since it is supplied with a useful glossary (a reprinting, incidentally, would have been a convenience to students in view of Hilton's importance in the development of English prose). But it came to seem that too many people would be completely put off by a first glance at it. It would have been a waste of time to produce a fresh modernization when I had the opportunity to use Mr Sherley-Price's; Hilton's *nuances* could have been preserved, perhaps, in particular instances, but this would have been more than offset, I feared, by a general loss in readability. It would be a pity not to give one example of Hilton's own style of writing (possibly in his very words):

'The lover of God seeth well that him needeth for to keep his bodily life with meat and drink as long as God will suffer them to be together. Then shall this be the discretion of the lover of Jhesu, as I understand, that hath feeling and working in love; that upon what manner that he may most keep his grace whole, and least be letted from working in it through taking of bodily sustenance, so shall he do. That manner meat that least letteth and least troubleth the heart and may keep the body in strength, be it flesh, be it fish, be it but bread and ale, that I trow the soul chooseth for to have if it may come thereby. For all the business of the soul is aye for to think on Jhesu with reverent love, without letting of anything, if that it might. And therefore since that it must needs somewhat be letted and hindered, the less it is letted and hindered by meat or drink or any other thing the liefer it is. It had liefer use the best meat and most of price that is under sun, if it less letted the keeping of his heart, than for to take but bread and water if that letted him more; for he hath no regard for to get him great meed for the pain of fasting and be put thereby from softness in heart. But all his business is for to keep his heart as stably as he may in the sight of Jhesu and in the feeling of His love.' (Book Two, Chapter 46 (39))

This good wine needs no bush.

6 ══════════════════════════ Hilton's reputation

Miss Kirchberger, in the first sentence of her Introduction, refers to Hilton as 'the greatest of our fourteenth-century mystical writers'. Miss Underhill seems to say, in effect, the same thing: 'Probably no English devotional work has had so wide and enduring an influence as *The Scale of Perfection* . . . perhaps the most wonderful descriptions of Christo-centric contemplation that exist. . . . In this worship of the Holy Name, with its penetrating intimacy, its spiritual realism, its poetic charm, we have perhaps the most precious treasure of mediaeval religion' (*op. cit.*, pp. vi, xxvi, xxvii). Miss Underhill justly remarks: 'As we become familiar with this book there gradually grows up in us the sense of contact with a soul of great depth and sweetness, at once shrewd and humble, ardent and practical: a religious realist of the noblest kind' (p. xxiv). When *The Scale* was printed in 1494, 'an honour accorded neither to Rolle nor Julian of Norwich', it became 'one of the favourite religious books of the laity' (p. vi). It is said that it was read at meals to the mother of Edward IV, and it was the munificent Lady Margaret, mother of Henry VII, who caused Wynkyn de Worde to print it. The manuscript on which Miss Underhill chiefly relied came from the London Charterhouse, and 'it is probably the actual volume which nourished the spiritual life of the saintly John Houghton' (p. xlvi), whose journey to his martyrdom was witnessed by St Thomas More from his window in the Tower and had so wonderful an effect on him (quite probably he used the same volume himself). And *The Scale* 'was evidently well known and much loved by the English Benedictines' (p. li); the notes on it by Dom Augustine Baker, the author of *Sancta Sophia*, are to be found among the manuscripts in the library of Downside Abbey.

Dr Gardner, however, wrote in her article: '*The Cloud* is a work of genius, *The Scale*, though beautiful, is not.' Professor Colledge says: 'It must, of course, be conceded that in *The Cloud* . . . the author is attempting something much more difficult than Hilton in *The Scale*', and he goes on to say: 'This is doubtless what was in Dr Gardner's mind . . . we may think it true to say that they display different kinds of genius. . . .' But what he is concerned to emphasize here is that, in his opinion, 'the achievement of *The Book of Privy Counsel* is unique' (*op. cit.*, p. 73). *The Book of Privy Counsel* was written, undoubtedly, by the author of *The Cloud*. Professor Colledge's opinion of it is surely justified. He did a great service in printing it in his anthology (it occupies forty of his pages). As I see it, this book teaches the doctrine of *The Cloud* in a way which is both acceptable and more encouraging. By the point at which it tells us that 'it must always be your intention and your wish in this exercise to feel God' (p. 180 of the anthology), we realize, I think, that it is in fact a super-intellectualism that the author is advocating: it is only the 'natural', discursive, intellect that has no place in this sort of prayer. And when we read, on the same page: 'you should forget to feel your own being as you feel the being of God', it causes us here no misgivings. The writing is even more impressive than it is in *The Cloud*. And certainly the unknown author of these two books undertook a peculiarly difficult task in grappling with such issues in the metaphysical language of 'being'. Hilton made no such attempt. It must be agreed that the two writers are equally astonishing, each in his own way. Hilton's scope is much wider, and his effect is cumulative: the other can rise to passages of a smouldering intensity which are in the highest degree distinctive and indeed (I suppose) incomparable.

But does Hilton's account go the whole way? Professor Knowles wrote: 'Hilton comes nearest [of the English mystics] to providing a complete guide to the spiritual life' but 'Hilton, again like *The Cloud*, does not touch upon the highest point to which the soul made perfect may attain; there is nothing to be set against the many chapters in *The Living Flame* and *The Spiritual Canticle* of St John of the Cross that describe the spiritual marriage and the life of the soul on even higher levels. The reader can scarcely doubt that Hilton himself had experience of the earlier stages, at least, which in the scheme of later mystical writers would be called the preparation of the soul for the spiritual betrothal' (pp. 198, 115). And again: 'Neither dwells in any detail on the highest degree of the contemplative life . . . most readers will feel sure that they were in fact contemplatives, but they will probably feel also that their range was far smaller than that of Ruysbroeck and the great Spaniards' (p. 192). I am quite incompetent to make such distinctions, and I cannot help suspecting that most readers will find themselves in the same case. But I would suggest that when Hilton declares his own incompetence we need not take it very seriously. It should be of interest to note that Professor Knowles's verdict is not that of Father Conrad Pepler, OP, to mention only one authority. In his valuable chapters on Hilton in *The English Religious Heritage* Father Pepler wrote: 'It is not difficult to trace in the works of Walter Hilton a direct line of prayer from its inception until it reaches the union of marriage with God' (p. 432) and, with particular reference to *The Scale*, Book Two, Chapter 48 (41): 'This is the language of the true mystic of all centuries, the language of St John of the Cross as much as of Hilton, the language of divine union in terms of marriage' (p. 442). What is certainly true is that towards the end of *The Scale* Hilton came to think that some things cannot be much talked about, by himself at any rate; he was not a poet like St John.

Whatever restrictions *The Scale* may be thought to exhibit, its importance for general purposes is undiminished. Here too I must refer to Father Pepler. There is a danger, he thinks, that 'those who base themselves exclusively on [St John's] *Ascent* are likely to leave out the problem of action and contemplation and so fall into the snare of regarding the two as independent ways to perfection. Hilton recalls his readers to the ancient and constant tradition that action is the beginning and belongs to the purgative and illuminative way but must eventually lead to the peaceful vision flowing from the contemplative life. That is why *The Scale* is of such value to many modern readers who have been nourished almost entirely on the Spanish mystical writers of the Renaissance' (*op. cit.*, p. 378). Again Dom Gerard Sitwell has written in an essay on Hilton published in *English Spiritual Writers* (Burns Oates, 1961): 'Hilton's treatise is very valuable and full of practical advice for those who are trying to lead a serious spiritual life but would by no means call themselves contemplatives.' This, for me, is what matters. And here I cannot forbear to quote from Ephrem Guy, a Downside monk who edited *The Scale* in 1869: 'Unfortunately the very name of Mysticism is apt to frighten off from the perusal of any avowed mystical treatise, a large class of devout and fervent souls, to whom a little instruction in the way of proceeding along the higher road of perfection, would be of untold utility . . . as Mystical Theology unless based upon Moral, would fall away into wild fanaticism, so Devotional Theology sinks into mere sentiment unless both its teachers and disciples ballast themselves with the solid and genuine principles of true Mysticism' (Preface, pp. vii, viii). Just for the record, since Miss Underhill (p. li) seems to have been in error on the point, Dom Ephrem used the printing of 1659, attributed to the Benedictine Serenus Cressy (of *John Inglesant*), the editor of *Sancta Sophia*.

At the beginning I proposed that Hilton is the most useful of our fourteenth-century mystics for the present time. Of the earliest of them, Richard Rolle, it is said on all hands that, despite the obvious genuineness of his magnificent enthusiasm, he is not as well-balanced a person as Hilton and so less reliable as a guide. Of the author of *The Cloud* and *The Book* (who is supposed, but by no means proved, to have come next in order of time), I need only add that, in my opinion, he is best read *after* a reading of *The Scale*, as supplementing in a most striking way some of its central themes—if possible, with the help of Professor Phyllis Hodgson's comments in the Introduction to her critical edition of *The Cloud* and *The Book* (Early English Text Society, 1947; '*The Cloud*,' she discreetly remarks on p. 22, 'is more concerned with the will and love, *Privy Counselling* [*The Book*] with the intelligence'). There remains Dame Julian of Norwich, who outlived Hilton by more than twenty years but may have written her *Revelations of Divine Love* after reading *The Scale*. I believe that we should profit more from her marvellous, if sometimes idiosyncratic, insights after reading *The Scale* ourselves. While Hilton has remained out of print, popular presentations of Rolle, of *The Cloud* and of Dame Julian have been appearing. The Penguin edition of *The Cloud* has been reprinted six times in the last ten years. There is thus an age-group for which *The Cloud* (but not *The Book*) has a considerable reputation while Hilton has virtually none. It seemed high time for someone to do something about this situation, even with the risks which attend a non-specialist's incursion into a field which might seem reserved for specialists.

II THE TEXT

BOOK ONE

Chapter 12

What unites Jesus to a man's soul, and what separates him from it

Jesus is united to a man's soul by goodwill and by a deep desire to possess him alone, and see him spiritually in his glory. The stronger this desire, the closer the union between Jesus and the soul: the weaker this desire, the looser the union. Any spirit or experience that weakens this desire and distracts the soul from constant thought of Jesus Christ and its proper aspiration for him will damage and disrupt this union between Jesus and the soul. It is therefore not of God, but the work of the devil. But if some spiritual experience or revelation fires the desire, draws the knot of love and devotion to Jesus more tightly, clarifies the soul's spiritual vision and knowledge, and makes the soul more humble, then it comes from God. From this you will understand that you may not deliberately allow your heart to depend on or derive all its pleasure from any sensible consolations of this kind even if they are good. Regard them as of little significance compared with the spiritual desire and constant thought of Jesus Christ, and do not allow your thoughts to become too engrossed in them.

Devote all your energies to prayer, so that your soul may come to a real perception of God; that is, that you may come to know the wisdom of God, the infinite might of our Lord Jesus Christ, his great goodness in himself and towards his creatures. For true contemplation consists in this, and not in these other matters. Thus St Paul says: *In caritate radicati et fundati, ut possitis comprehendere cum omnibus sanctis, quae sit longitudo, et latitudo, sublimitas, et profundum* (Eph. 3:17). Be rooted and grounded in love—not in order to experience sound or sweet savours or other physical sensations—but that with all the saints you may know and experience something of the greatness of the infinite being of God, the wideness of his wonderful love and goodness, the height of his almighty majesty, and the boundless depths of his wisdom.

2 ═══════════════════════════════════ Chapter 24

On prayer as an aid towards purity of heart and other virtues

[. . .] The purpose of prayer is not to inform our Lord what you desire, for he knows all your needs. It is to render you able and ready to receive the grace which our Lord will freely give you. This grace cannot be experienced until you have been refined and purified by the fire of desire in devout prayer. For although prayer is not the cause for which our Lord gives grace, it is nevertheless the means by which grace, freely given, comes to the soul.

You may now perhaps desire to learn how to pray, to what you should direct your thoughts during prayer, and what form of prayer is best for you to use [. . .]

3 ═══════════════════════════════════ Chapter 25

How we should pray, and the matter of our thoughts in prayer

When you pray, detach your heart from all earthly things, and use all your efforts to withdraw your mind from them, so that it may be stripped and freed of these things and rise continually to Jesus Christ. You will never be able to see him as he is in his divinity, nor can your imagination conceive of him as he is; but devout and constant recollection of the humility of his precious humanity will enable you to experience his goodness and the grace of his divinity. If, when you pray, your heart is lightened, helped, and freed from the burden of all worldly thoughts and affections, and rises up in the power of the spirit to a spiritual delight in his presence so that you are scarcely conscious of earthly things or are little distracted by them, then you are praying well. For prayer is nothing other than the ascent of the heart to God, and its withdrawal from all earthly thoughts. Therefore prayer is compared to fire, which of its own nature always leaves the earth and leaps into the air. Similarly, prayerful desire, when touched and kindled by the spiritual fire of God, constantly leaps upwards to him from whom it comes.

4 ———————————————— Chapter 27

How the vocal prayers ordained by God or approved by Holy Church are best for those who are under obligation to use them, as well as for those who are beginners in prayer

I will now give you my opinion on the second point: namely, how to know what kind of prayer is best. You should understand that there are three degrees of prayer. The first is vocal prayer, whether enjoined by God, as is the *Our Father*, or more generally by Holy Church [. . .]

This form of prayer is usually more helpful than any other spiritual exercise to a person in the beginning of his spiritual life. For unless he is granted especial grace, a person is at first undisciplined and worldly, and he cannot meditate on spiritual things because his soul is not yet cleansed of his former sin. And so I think it best for such to use the *Our Father*, the *Hail Mary*, and to recite the Psalms. For one who cannot readily pray with the spirit, because the feet of his knowledge are lamed by sin, needs to have a firm staff to support him. This staff is the particular forms of vocal prayer ordained by God and Holy Church to help men's souls. By this prayer the soul of a worldly man, who is always relapsing into worldly thoughts and carnal desires, is raised up and supported as if by a staff. He is nourished by the sweet words of the prayer as a child is nourished with milk. And he is guided by it so that his mind does not fall into errors and foolish fancies. There is no possibility of a mistake in this form of prayer for anyone who will patiently and humbly persevere in it.

The second degree of prayer, which follows the impulses of devotion without any set form

The second degree of prayer is vocal, but employs no particular set form. This is when anyone by the grace of God experiences the grace of devotion, and out of this devotion speaks to God as though he were bodily in his presence, using such words as best express his feelings and come to his mind at the time. He may recall his sins and wretchedness, the malice and deceits of the devil, or the goodness and mercy of God. Out of the desire of his heart he calls on our Lord as a man will do when in peril among his enemies or in sickness, showing his hurts to God as he would to a physician, and saying as David said: *Eripe me de inimicis meis, Deus meus* (Ps. 59:1). 'Deliver me from my enemies, O God.' Or else, *Sana animam meam, quia peccavi tibi* (Ps. 41:4). 'Heal my soul, for I have sinned against Thee.' Or such other petition as comes to his mind. He knows the greatness of God's goodness, grace, and mercy, and wishes to love him with all his heart, and to thank him with such words and psalms as will fittingly express his love and praise of God. As David said: *Confitemini Domino quoniam bonus, quoniam in saeculum misericordia ejus* (Ps. 136:1). 'Love and praise the Lord, for he is good and merciful.' And he will use any other prayers that he is moved to say.

How this kind of prayer is very pleasing to God, and wounds a man's soul with the sword of love

This kind of prayer is very pleasing to God because it springs directly from the heart, and is therefore never offered without some reward of grace [. . .] Whoever receives this gift of fervour from God should withdraw from the company of other people and be alone, so that it may not be interrupted. Let whoever has it retain it while he can, for its fervour will not remain long. For whenever grace comes powerfully it imposes a great strain on the spirit, even while it brings joy. It is also a great strain on the body if experienced often, for at the mighty surge of grace the body stirs and moves about like that of a madman or drunkard who can find no ease. This is one effect of passionate love, which in its violence utterly destroys all love of earthly things and wounds the soul with the sword of joyful love, so that the body collapses, unable to bear it. So potent is God's touch on the soul that were the most wicked sinner on earth to be touched only once by this sharp sword, he would thenceforward be a graver and better man. He would loathe all sinful lusts and desires, and cease to be attracted by the worldly things that had once been his chief delight.

7 ═══════════════════ Chapter 3²

On the third degree of prayer, which is in the heart alone and is without words

The third degree of prayer is in the heart alone; it is without words, and is accompanied by great peace and tranquillity of body and soul. One who wishes to pray in this way must have a pure heart, for the gift comes only to those who, either through long bodily and spiritual effort, or through such sudden visitations of love as I have described, have attained quietness of soul. As a result, their affections become wholly spiritual, their hearts are continually at prayer, and they can love and praise God without serious hindrance from temptations or worldly thoughts [. . .] Of this kind of prayer St Paul says: *Nam si orem lingua, spiritus meus orat, mens autem mea sine fructu est. Quid ergo? orabo et spiritu, orabo et mente; psallam spiritu, psallam et mente* (I Cor. 14:14). Meaning, that if I pray with my tongue only, by an effort of will, the prayer is commendable but my soul is not satisfied, because it cannot taste the fruit of spiritual joy through the understanding. 'What shall I do then?' asks St Paul. And he answers: I will pray with spiritual effort and desire. I will also pray more inwardly in my spirit without effort, and will taste the sweetness of the love and sight of God. It is this perception and experience of the love of God that will satisfy my soul. This—as I understand—was how St Paul prayed [. . .]

8

=== Chapter 33

How to deal with distraction in prayer

But you may now complain that I am speaking in over-exalted terms about this kind of prayer, since it is easy enough to talk about it, but by no means easy to practise. You state that you are unable to pray in the devout and wholehearted way that I have described. For when you wish to raise your heart to God in prayer, many useless thoughts fill your mind, of what you have done, of what you are going to do, of what others are doing, and such like. These thoughts hinder and distract you so much that you feel no joy, peace, or devotion in your prayer. And often the more you struggle to collect your thoughts, the more obstinate and wandering they become. Sometimes this lasts from the beginning to the end of your prayer, and you think all your efforts are lost.

When you say that I spoke in over-exalted terms about prayer, I frankly admit that I am describing something that I cannot practise. Nevertheless, I do so because we ought to understand how to pray well. And since we cannot pray well, we should humbly acknowledge our weakness and cry to God for mercy. Our Lord himself told us this when he said: *Diliges Dominum Deum tuum ex toto corde tuo, ex tota anima tua, et ex omnibus viribus tuis* (Luke 10:27). You shall love God with all your heart, and all your soul, and all your strength. It is impossible for anyone to fulfil this command perfectly in this life, but our Lord nevertheless bids us love in this way. And its purpose, as St Bernard says, is that we should recognize our weakness and humbly cry for mercy, and we shall receive it. However, I will give you my advice on this question.

When you pray, begin by directing your will and intention to God as briefly, fully, and purely as possible; then continue as well as you can. And although your original purpose may seem largely frustrated, do not be distressed and angry with yourself or impatient with God because he does not give you feelings of devotion and spiritual joy that you imagine he gives to others. Recognize in this your own weakness, accept it readily, and humbly hold to your prayer, poor as it is, firmly trusting that our Lord in his mercy will make it good and profitable, more than you know or feel. For remember that your good intention is accepted in discharge of your duty, and will be rewarded like any other good deed done in charity, even though your mind was distracted when you did it. Therefore do your duty, and allow our Lord to do what he will; do not try to teach him his part. And although you know yourself to be thoughtless and negligent, yet for this, as well as for all venial sins that cannot be avoided in this wretched life, lift up your heart to God, acknowledge your sinfulness, and plead for mercy with firm trust in his forgiveness. Give up struggling against yourself, and do not worry about it any longer, as though you could force yourself not to have these feelings. Leave your prayer and turn to some other good occupation, either spiritual or physical, and resolve to do better another time. Although you fail another time in the same way—even a hundred or a thousand times—yet do as I have said, and all will be well. Furthermore, a soul who never finds peace of heart in prayer but has to struggle against distracting and troublesome thoughts all her life, provided that she keeps herself in humility and charity in other ways, shall receive full reward in heaven for all her trouble.

9 ═══════════════════════════ Chapter 41

That everyone should know the extent of his own gift, and always desire a better, so that he can accept it when God wills to give it

The holy fathers in years gone by have taught us that we should know the extent of our gift and labour to perfect it, without pretending to have more than we know ourselves to possess. We may always desire the best gifts, but we may not always obtain them, because we have not yet received the grace necessary for them. A hound that only runs after the hare because he sees other hounds run rests when he is tired or returns home. But if he runs because he sees the hare, he will not stop until he has caught it, tired though he may be. Our spiritual progress is very similar. Whoever has some grace, however small, and wilfully neglects to develop it, but sets himself to obtain some other grace that he has not yet been granted merely because he sees or hears that other people possess it, may indeed run for a while until he is weary, but will then return home again. And unless he is careful, he may in consequence injure his powers before he gets home. But whoever uses such grace as he has, and aspires after greater grace with humble and constant prayer, provided he remains humble, may safely pursue his quest once he feels moved to follow after the grace which he desired. Therefore desire from God as strongly as you may, without measure or discretion, all that belongs to his love and to the joy of heaven; for whoever desires most of God will receive most from him. Do your utmost, and ask God's mercy for whatever you cannot do. St Paul seems to refer to this when he says: *Unusquisque habet donum suum ex Deo, alius autem sic, alius vero sic* (I Cor. 7:7). *Item unicuique nostrum data est gratia secundum mensuram donationis Christi* (Eph. 4:7). *Divisiones gratiarum sunt, alii daturse rmo sapientiae: alii sermo scientiae* (I Cor. 12:4-8). *Item ut sciamus quae a Deo donata sunt nobis* (I Cor. 2:12). St Paul says that each mean has his gift from God, one man this, another that. For to each man who will be saved is given grace according to the measure of Christ's gift. We therefore need to know the gifts given us by God, so that we may use them, for by these we shall be saved [. . .]

10 ——————————————— Chapter 42

That a man should study to know his own soul and its powers, and to destroy the roots of sin in it

Nevertheless, there is one work in which it is both very necessary and helpful to engage, and which—so far as human efforts are concerned —is a highway leading to contemplation. This is for a person to enter into himself, and to understand his own soul with all its powers, virtues, and sins. In this interior examination you will come to recognize the honour and dignity proper to the soul at its creation, and the wretchedness and error into which you have fallen through sin. This realization will bring with it a heartfelt desire to recover the dignity and honour which you have lost. You will be filled with disgust and contempt for yourself, and with a firm resolve to humble yourself and to destroy everything that stands between you and that dignity and joy. Those who wish to make rapid progress in this task will at first find it hard and painful, for it is a conflict in the soul against the root of all sins great and small, and this is nothing other than a false and misplaced love of self. From this love, as St Augustine says, springs every kind of sin, both mortal and venial. Indeed, until this root is completely dug up and exposed, and as it were almost dried up by the casting out of all loves and fears of the world and the flesh, the soul can never experience the burning love of Jesus Christ. It cannot enjoy the closeness of his gracious presence, nor can its understanding be opened to a clear insight into spiritual things. This task, however, is necessary if a person is to detach his heart and mind from the love of all earthly things, from vain thoughts, and from material considerations, and from misplaced love of self, so that his soul may find no satisfaction in them. Then, in so far as the soul cannot find its satisfaction in the love and sight of Jesus Christ, it is bound to suffer pain. This task is difficult and arduous to a degree; nevertheless, I am sure that it is the way which Christ teaches in the Gospel to those who wish to love him perfectly, saying: *Contendite intrare per angustam portam: quia arcta est via quae ducit ad vitam, et pauci inveniunt eam* (Matt. 7 : 14). Strive to enter by the narrow gate, for the way that leads to heaven is narrow, and few men find it. And how narrow this way is our Lord tells us in another place: *Si quis vult venire post me, abneget semetipsum, et tollat crucem suam, et sequatur me* (Matt. 16 : 24). *Item qui odit animam suam in hoc mundo, in vitam aeternam custodit eam* (John 12 : 25). That is to say: Whoever wishes to follow me, let him forsake himself and hate his own soul. In other words, forsake all worldly love and hate his own bodily life and the vain desires of his bodily senses for love of me. And let him take the cross—that is, suffer the pain of this world awhile—and then follow me in the contemplation of my humanity and my divinity. This way is so strait and narrow that no earthly thing may pass through it, for it demands the slaying of all sin. As St Paul says: *Mortificate membra vestra quae sunt super terram, immunditiam, libidinem, concupiscientiam malam* (Col. 3 : 5). Slay your earthly members—not the bodily members, but those of the soul—such as impurity, lust, and immoderate love of self and earthly things. Therefore, as your efforts hitherto have been to withstand grave material sins and open temptations of the devil, which originate outside yourself, you must now undertake this spiritual task within yourself, and, so far as you are able, destroy and break up the roots of sin in yourself. I will now give you what advice I can, so that you may more readily bring this about.

II ⸻ Chapter 43

How a man should know the high estate and dignity first given to his soul by God, and the wretched misfortune into which it has fallen by sin

The soul of man is a life consisting of three powers, memory, understanding, and will. It is made in the image and likeness of the blessed Trinity, whole, perfect, and righteous. For the mind was created strong and steadfast by the virtue of the Father, so that it might hold fast to him, neither forgetting him nor being distracted and hindered by created things; and so it has the likeness of the Father. The understanding was made clear and bright, without error or obscurity, and as perfect as might be in a body not glorified; and so it has the likeness of the Son, who is eternal wisdom. The will and its affections was made pure, rising like a flame towards God without love of the flesh or of any creatures, by the sovereign goodness of God the Holy Spirit; and so it has the likeness of the Holy Spirit, who is holy love. So man's soul, which may be called a created trinity, was made complete in the mind, sight, and love of the uncreated and blessed Trinity, who is God. This is the dignity and honourable state natural to man's soul at its creation. This state was yours in Adam before man's first sin; but when Adam sinned, choosing to love and delight in himself and in creatures, he lost all his honour and dignity, and you also in him, and he fell from that blessed Trinity into a vile, dark, and wretched trinity: that is, into forgetfulness and ignorance of God, and into a debasing and deliberate love of himself. For as David says in the psalms: *Homo, cum in honore esset, non intellexit: comparatus est jumentis insipientibus, et similis factus est illis* (Ps. 49:20). When man had honour he did not know it; therefore he lost it and became like a beast. See, then, the present wretched plight of your soul. Your mind, once firmly fixed on God, has now forgotten him and tries to find satisfaction in creatures, first in one and then another; but it can never find true peace, because it has lost him in whom alone true peace may be found. Your will also, once pure, taking a joy and delight in spiritual things, has now turned to a degraded love of self, of creatures, and of material pleasures. As a result your senses are corrupted by greed and impurity, and your mind by pride, vainglory, and covetousness. So deep is this corruption that you can hardly do anything good without being tainted by vainglory; and you can scarcely direct any of your senses to some desirable object without your heart becoming obsessed and inflamed by a vain desire to possess it. This drives from your heart and makes impossible all spiritual experience of, and desire for, the love of God. Everyone who lives by the spirit knows this well. It is the spiritual misery and mischief caused by man's first sin, to say nothing of all the other wickedness and sin that you have deliberately added to it [. . .]

I2 ═══════════════════════════ Chapter 46

How Jesus is to be sought, desired, and found

[. . .] If, then, you feel a great longing in your heart for Jesus—either by the remembrance of his name Jesus, or of any other word, prayer, or deed—and if this longing is so strong that its force drives out of your heart all other thoughts and desires of the world and the flesh, then you are indeed seeking your Lord Jesus. And if, when you feel this desire for God, for Jesus—for it is all one—you are helped and strengthened by a supernatural might so strong that it is changed into love and affection, spiritual savour and sweetness and knowledge of truth, so that for the time your mind is set on no created thing, nor on any feeling or stirring of vainglory nor self-love nor any other evil affections (for these cannot appear at such a time) so that you are enclosed in Jesus alone, resting in him with the warmth of tender love, then you have found something of Jesus. Not Jesus as he is, but an inward sight of him; and the more fully you find him, the more you will desire him. So whatever form of prayer, meditation, or activity leads you to the highest and purest desire for him, and to the deepest experience of him, will be the means by which you may best seek and find him. Therefore, if you will consider what you have lost and what you seek, lift up your mind and heartfelt desire to Jesus Christ, even though you are blind and can see nothing of his Godhead. Say to yourself that it is he whom you have lost, and he alone whom you desire to have, that you may be with him where he is, since there is no other joy, no other bliss in heaven or in earth except in him. And even though you feel his nearness through the gift of devotion or knowledge or in any other way, do not rest content with this feeling as though you had fully found Jesus. Forget what you have found, and always desire Jesus more and more, so that you may find him more fully, as though you had so far found nothing. For consider this, that however great your experience of him may be—even though you were carried up in spirit to the third heaven like St Paul—you have not yet known Jesus as he is in his glory. However deep your knowledge and experience of him, he utterly transcends it. Therefore, if you wish to find him as he is in the realms of love and joy, let your soul never cease to long for him in this present life.

13 ======= Chapter 47

How profitable it is to have the desire for Jesus

I would rather feel in my heart a true and pure desire for my Lord Jesus Christ, although I had very little spiritual knowledge of him, than perform all the bodily penances of all men living, or enjoy visions and revelations of angels, hear sweet sounds, or experience any other pleasurable outward sensations, were they unaccompanied by this desire. In short, all the joys of heaven and earth would have no attraction for me unless I might also have this desire for Jesus. I think that the prophet David felt this when he wrote: *Quid enim mihi est in caelo? et a te quid volui super terram?* (Ps. 73:23). Lord, what have I in heaven but thee? And what can I desire on earth but thee? As though he had said: Lord Jesus, what heavenly joy can satisfy me, unless I desire thee while I am on earth, and love thee when I come to heaven? Meaning, none indeed! Therefore, if you wish to have any inward knowledge of him, whether in body or soul, seek nothing but an earnest desire for his grace and his merciful presence, and recognize that your heart can find no satisfaction in anything outside him. This was David's desire, when he said: *Concupivit anima mea desiderare justificationes tuas in omni tempore* (Ps. 119:20). Lord, my soul longed for the desire of thy righteousness. Therefore seek desire by desire, as David did. And if in your prayers and meditations your desire leads you to feel the inward presence of Jesus Christ in your soul, hold firmly to it in your heart, so that you do not lose it: then if you should fall, you may soon find him again.

Therefore seek Jesus whom you have lost. He wishes to be sought, and longs to be found, for he himself says: *Omnis qui quaerit, invenit* (Matt. 7:8). Every one who seeks shall find. The search is arduous, but the finding is full of joy. Therefore if you wish to find him, follow the counsel of the wise man, who said: *Si quaesieris quasi pecuniam sapientiam, et sicut thesauros effodieris illum; tunc intelliges timorem Domini, et scientiam Dei invenies* (Prov. 2:4). If you seek wisdom—which is Jesus—like silver and gold, and dig deep for it, you shall find it. You must dig deep in your heart, for he is hidden there, and you must cast out utterly all love and desire of earthly things, and all sorrows and fears with regard to them. In this way you shall find Jesus the true wisdom.

14 ——————————————— Chapter 48

Where and how Jesus is to be sought and found

Be like the woman in the Gospel, of whom our Lord said: *Quae mulier habens drachmas decem, si perdiderit unam, nonne accendit lucernam, et everrit domum suam, et quaerit diligenter donec inveniat eam? Et cum invenerit, convocat amicos suos, dicens; Congratulamini mihi, quia inveni drachmam quam perdideram* (Luke 15:8). What woman is there who will not light a lamp, and turn her house upside down, and search until she finds it? Implying: none. And when she has found it, she calls her friends to her and says: Rejoice with me, for I have found the coin that I had lost. This coin is Jesus, whom you have lost: if you wish to find him, light the lamp of God's word. As David says: *Lucerna pedibus meis verbum tuum* (Ps. 119:105). Lord, thy word is a lamp to my feet. By this lamp you will see where he is, and how you may find him. You may light another lamp if you wish, which is your reason, for our Lord says: *Lucerna corporis tui oculus tuus* (Matt. 6:22). The light of your body is the eye. Similarly it may be said that the lamp of the soul is the reason, by which the soul may come to see all spiritual things. With this lamp you will certainly find Jesus if you hold it up from underneath the measure. As our Lord says: *Nemo accendit lucernam et ponit eam sub modio, sed super candelabrum* (Matt. 5:15). No one lights a lamp in order to set it under a measure, but on a lampstand: that is to say, your mind must not be engrossed in worldly activities, useless thoughts, and earthly desires, but must always aspire above all earthly things to the inward vision of Jesus Christ. If you do this, you will see all the dust, dirt, and small blemishes in your house, that is, all the worldly loves and fears within your soul. Yet not all, for as David says: *Delicta quis intelligit?* (Ps. 19:12). Who may know all his sin? Meaning, no one. Cast out all these sins from your heart, sweep your soul clean with the broom of the fear of God, wash it with your tears, and you shall find your coin, Jesus. He is the coin, he is the penny, and he is your heritage. It is easier to describe this coin than to find it, for the search is not the work of an hour or a day, but of many days and years, and it demands both bodily toil and spiritual effort. But if you do not give up, but search diligently, sorrow deeply, grieve silently, and humble yourself until tears of pain and anguish flow because you have lost Jesus your treasure: then at length and when he wills it you shall find him. And if you find him as I have said—that is, if you are able with a pure conscience to feel the close and peaceful presence of our blessed Lord Jesus Christ, given as a foreshadowing and glimpse of him as he is— then you may if you wish call your friends to sing and make merry with you because you have found your coin, Jesus.

15 ═══════════════════════ Chapter 49

Where Jesus is lost, and through his mercy found again

See now the courtesy and mercy of Jesus. You have lost him. But where? In your own house; that is, in your soul. If you had lost him outside your own house—that is, if you had lost the power of reason through original sin—you would never have found him again. But he left you your reason, and so he is within your soul, and will never be lost outside it. Nevertheless you are no nearer to him until you have found him. He is within you, although he is lost to you; but you are not in him until you have found him. In this, too, is his mercy, that he would suffer himself to be lost only where he may be found. There is no need to travel to Rome or Jerusalem to search for him: but turn your thoughts into your own soul where he is hidden, and seek him there. For as the prophet says: *Vere tu es deus absconditus* (Isa. 45:15). Truly, Lord, thou art a hidden God. And Christ himself says in the Gospel: *Simile est regnum caelorum thesauro abscondito in agro: quem qui invenit homo, prae gaudio illius vadit, et vendit universa quae habet, et emit agrum illum* (Matt. 13:44). The kingdom of heaven is like a treasure hidden in a field, which when a man finds, for joy of it he goes and sells all that he has and buys that field. Jesus is the treasure hidden in your soul. If you could find him in your soul, and your soul in him, I am sure that you would gladly give up the love of all earthly things in order to have him. Jesus sleeps spiritually in your heart as he once slept bodily in the ship with his disciples. But they, fearing to perish, awoke him, and he quickly saved them from the tempest. Therefore rouse him as they did by prayer, and wake him with the loud cry of your desire, and he will quickly rise and help you.

16 ⎯⎯⎯⎯⎯⎯⎯⎯⎯⎯⎯⎯⎯⎯ Chapter 51

That humility and charity are the especial livery of Jesus, through which man's soul is reformed to his likeness

Prepare yourself, therefore, to be clothed with his likeness—that is, in humility and charity which are his livery—and then he will admit you to his friendship and show you his secrets. He himself said to his disciples: *Qui diligit me diligetur a Patre meo, et manifestabo ei meipsum* (John 14:21). Whoever loves me shall be loved by my Father, and I will show myself to him. There is no virtue that you can acquire or work that you can do that will make you like our Lord without humility and charity, for these two are God's especial livery. This is clearly seen in the Gospel, where our Lord speaks of humility: *Discite a me, quia mitis sum et humilis corde.* Learn of me, he says, not to go barefoot, or fast in the desert for forty days, or choose disciples, but learn from me humility, for I am gentle and humble of heart. And of charity he says: *Hoc est praeceptum meum: ut diligatis invicem sicut dilexi vos. Item in hoc cognoscent homines quia discipuli mei estis, si dilectionem habueritis ad invicem* (John 13:34). This is my commandment, that you love one another as I have loved you; for in this shall men know you for my disciples. Not because you work miracles, or cast out devils, or preach and teach, but because each of you loves the other in charity. If you will be like him, be humble and loving. And charity means that you must have a true love for your fellow-Christian.

17 ⎯⎯⎯⎯⎯⎯⎯⎯⎯⎯⎯⎯⎯⎯ Chapter 65

That it is a great achievement to love men sincerely while hating their sin

It is no achievement to watch and fast until your head aches and your body sickens, nor to go to Rome and Jerusalem on your bare feet, nor to rush about preaching as though you expected to convert everybody. Nor is it an achievement to build churches and chapels, to feed the poor, or to build hospitals. But it is a great achievement for a man to be able to love his fellow-Christian in charity, and to be discerning enough to hate his sin and yet love the sinner. For although all the above actions are good in themselves, they are done by good men and bad alike, for everyone could do them if he had the desire and the means. So I do not consider it any achievement to do what everyone can do. But only a good man can love his fellow-Christian in charity while hating his sin, and he can only do it by the grace of God and not through his own efforts. As St Paul says: *Caritas Dei diffusa est in cordibus nostris per Spiritum Sanctum, qui datus est nobis* (Rom. 5:5). The love of God is shed abroad in our hearts by the Holy Spirit which is given to us. It is therefore the more precious and the more difficult to come by. Without this all other good actions do not make a man good or worthy of heaven: this alone can make him good and his actions worthy of reward. All other gifts of God are common to good and bad alike, but this gift of charity is granted only to good and chosen souls.

18 ———————————————— Chapter 70

How to ascertain whether you love your fellow-Christian, and how to follow Christ's example in this matter

If you are not moved to anger and open dislike of a person, and feel no secret hatred which makes you despise, humiliate, or belittle him, then you are in perfect charity with your fellow-Christian. And if, the more he shames or harms you in word or act, the more pity and compassion you feel towards him, as you would feel towards one who was out of his right mind, then you are in perfect charity. And if you feel that you cannot find it in your heart to hate him, knowing love to be good in itself, but pray for him, help him, and desire his amendment —not only in words as hypocrites can do, but with heartfelt love— then you are in perfect charity with your fellow-Christian. St Stephen possessed this perfect charity when he prayed for those who stoned him to death. And Christ called for this charity in all who desire to follow him perfectly when he said: *Diligite inimicos vestros, benefacite his qui oderunt vos, orate pro persequentibus et calumniatoribus* (Matt. 5:44). Love your enemies and do good to those who hate you; pray for those who persecute and slander you. Therefore, if you desire to follow Christ, imitate him in this matter. Learn to love your enemies and all sinners, for they are all your fellow-Christians. Remember how Christ loved Judas, who was both his deadly enemy and a wicked man. How patient Christ was with him, how kindly, how courteous and humble to one whom he knew to be worthy of damnation. Despite this he chose him to be his apostle, and sent him to preach with the other apostles. He gave him power to work miracles, he showed him the same loving friendship in word and deed as the other apostles. He washed his feet, he fed him with his precious body, and taught him as he did the other apostles. He did not openly expose or rebuke him, nor did he despise or speak ill of him, although he might justly have done all these things. And to crown his crimes, at Jesus' arrest Judas kissed him and called him his friend. Christ showed all this charity to one whom he knew to be a traitor; yet in everything that he did there was no pretence or insincerity, but pure love and true charity. For although Judas, because of his wickedness, was unworthy to receive any gift from God or any sign of love, it was nevertheless right and fitting that our Lord should show himself in his true nature. For he is love and goodness, and therefore shows love and goodness towards all his creatures as he did towards Judas. I do not say that he loved Judas for his sins, or that he loved him as one of his chosen, as he loved St Peter. But he loved him inasmuch as he was his creature, and gave him proofs of his love, if only he could have responded to them and amended.

[. . .] Anyone who thinks himself a perfect follower of Christ's teaching and way of life—as some do, inasmuch as they preach and teach and are poor in worldly goods as Christ was—but who cannot follow Christ in having love and charity towards all, both good and bad, friends and foes, without pretence or flattery, contempt, anger, or spiteful criticism, is indeed deceiving himself. The more closely that he thinks he is following the way of Christ, the further he is from it; for Christ himself said to those who wished to be his disciples: *Hoc est praeceptum meum, ut diligatis invicem sicut dilexi vos* (John 13:34). This is my commandment, that you love one another as I have loved you. For if you love as I loved, then you are my disciples.

But now you may ask, 'How am I to love the bad as well as the good?' I reply that you must love both good and bad with charity, although not for the same reason; and I will now explain how you are to love your fellow-Christian as yourself. Now you must love yourself only in God and for God. You love yourself in God when you are in a state of grace: but you love yourself solely because you love the goodness and virtue that God gives you. Then you love yourself in God, because you do not love yourself, but God. You love yourself because God loves you, and were you in a state of mortal sin and longed to be made good and virtuous, you would not love yourself as you are, but as you would wish to be. It is exactly in this way that you should love your fellow-Christians. If they are good and holy, you must love them in God with charity, for the reason that they *are* good and holy; for then you love God's goodness and righteousness in them, and you love them more than if they were in a state of mortal sin. As for your enemies, and others who are clearly not in a state of grace, you must love them too, not for what they are, nor as if they were good and holy, for they are not; but you must love them for God's sake, hoping that they will become good and holy. You are not to hate anything in them except whatever is contrary to righteousness, and that is sin. This, as I understand it, is the teaching of St Augustine. Only one who is sincerely humble, or desires to be, is capable of loving his fellow-Christian.

BOOK TWO

19 ————————————————— Chapter 10

How one whose soul is completely restored to the image of God makes every effort to avoid sin and keep himself in perfect charity with God and his neighbour

Most of God's chosen lead their lives reformed in faith alone. They are resolved to avoid all mortal sins, to keep themselves in love and charity with their neighbours, and to obey God's commandments to the best of their knowledge. And whenever evil feelings of pride, envy, anger, lust, or any other grievous sin rise in their hearts, they steel their wills to resist and reject them. Should they involuntarily commit some venial fault through frailty or ignorance, they are so troubled in conscience that they cannot rest until they have confessed and received forgiveness. I am sure that all who live in this way are reformed in faith to the image of God [. . .]

20 ————————————————— Chapter 11

How reformed souls need to fight constantly against temptations to sin; and how a soul may know whether it yields to temptation or not

This reformation in faith is easy to acquire, but not so easy to maintain, so that anyone who is truly reformed to God's likeness must devote much effort to keeping this likeness whole and pure, so that it does not degenerate into the image of sin through weakness of will. A reformed Christian dare not be idle or thoughtless, because the image of sin grips him firmly and constantly offers sinful suggestions, so that unless he is very watchful it is very easy to assent and fall. So he must be always fighting the evil suggestions of this wicked image, for he cannot come to terms with it or comply with its unlawful demands. If he does so, he deceives himself; but if he fights against it he need have little fear of yielding to it, for the struggle itself will dispel any false sense of security. It is right that a man should be at peace with all things except the devil and this sinful image, against which he must fight constantly in mind and body until he has overcome them. But he will not entirely overcome them in this life, while he carries this image with its evil influence within him. I do not deny that by the grace of God it is possible to win the upper hand over this image, to the extent that the soul will not follow or assent to its temptations; but it is not possible to be liberated from it entirely, for no one can avoid feeling the pull of evil suggestions, bodily desires, or vain thoughts in this life [. . .]

21 ———————————————— Chapter 13

On three types of people: those who are reformed, those who are unreformed, and those who are reformed both in faith and feeling

You will realize from what I have already said that people are of various types according to the varying states of their souls. Some are not reformed to the likeness of God, and some are reformed only in faith, while some are reformed both in faith and feeling.

For you must understand that the soul has two faculties. One is called sensibility, that is, the faculty of perception through the senses, which man shares with the animals. When this sensibility is not rightly directed and controlled, the image of sin arises; for if the senses are not ruled by the reason, the result is sin. The other faculty is called reason, and this itself has two powers, the higher and the lower reason. The higher may be termed male, since it should exercise control, and it is in this faculty that God's likeness exists, for it is only through this faculty that the soul knows and loves him. The lower faculty may be termed female, and should obey the higher reason as woman obeys man. Its function is to understand and control mundane things, to employ them with discretion as necessary, and to reject whatever is not essential. It must always watch, respect and follow the higher rational faculty. Now a man who lives only to gratify his bodily desires like an unreasoning animal, and who has neither knowledge of God nor desire for virtue and holy living, but is blinded by pride, gnawed by envy, dominated by greed, and corrupted by lust and other grave sins, is not reformed to the likeness of God. For such a man is entirely satisfied with and subject to the image of sin. But one who fears God and refuses to obey the dangerous impulses of the senses keeps control over worldly things, and makes it his aim to please God in all that he does. In this way the soul is reformed to the likeness of God in faith, and although it experiences the same temptations as the other soul, they cannot harm it since it does not surrender to them. But a soul which receives grace to resist all sensual temptations, both mortal and venial, and is not even disturbed by them, is reformed in feeling. For it follows the higher powers of reason, and is enabled to see God and spiritual things, as I shall explain later.

22 ═══════════════════════════ Chapter 14

How sinners come to resemble the animals, and are known to be lovers of this world

Wretched is the man who does not recognize the true worth of his soul, and has no wish to do so. For with the exception of the angels, whom it resembles, the soul is the highest of God's creations, and is superior to all other incarnate beings. Therefore man cannot find true rest except in God, and he should love and desire him alone, seeking only to be reformed to his likeness. But because he does not understand this, man tries to find rest and pleasure in creatures inferior to himself. Yet man acts contrary to nature and reason if he leaves God, the supreme good and source of all life, unsought, unloved, unknown, and unworshipped, and seeks rest and pleasure in the passing pleasures of the world. But this is what is done by all who love this world, and who seek happiness in this wretched life alone. Some find pleasure in pride and conceit, and having lost all reverence for God, they labour night and day to win the honour and praise of the world. Nothing matters to them so long as they win it and excel all others, whether in scholarship or technical skill, in reputation and fame, in riches and respect, in influence and authority, in estate and dignity. Some take delight in wealth, and make it their sole object to amass vast possessions. Their hearts are so set on this that they think of nothing but how to obtain it. Some love to gratify their bodily cravings in gluttony and lust, some in one way and some in another. And those who act in this vile manner degrade man's noble nature, and lower themselves to the level of beasts.

Pride turns a man into a lion, for he wishes to be feared and respected by everyone, and will not allow anyone to thwart his wishes by word or act. And if anyone resists his presumption he is furious, and sets on him like a lion does on a lesser beast. One who behaves in this way is no true man, and is acting contrary to man's true nature, so that he is changed into a lion. Envy and anger turn men into dogs. They bark at their neighbours, and bite them with wicked and malicious words; they harass those who have done them no harm, and harm them in body and soul contrary to God's laws. Some people become like asses, because they are slothful in the service of God, and unwilling to show any kindness to their neighbour. They are ready enough to hurry away to Rome for worldly profit and honours, or to win popular approval. But when it is a matter of spiritual gain, of the good of their own souls, or of God's glory, they are soon bored. They do not really want these things, and if they do anything at all, they only make a grudging gesture. Some people are so obstinately ignorant and ill-mannered that they are like swine. They have no fear of God, and only seek to gratify the lusts and desires of the body. They have no respect for the dignity of human nature, and make no attempt to be guided by reason or to control the irrational impulses of their physical nature. When bodily temptation arises, they yield to it at once, and revel in it like swine. Treacherous and covetous people who rob their neighbours of their worldly goods by threats and oppression become like ravening wolves. False and deceitful people who live by trickery and guile become like foxes [. . .]

How those who love this world hinder the reformation of their souls in various ways

But certain of these people say: 'I would gladly love God, be good, and renounce love of the world if I could, but I have not the grace to do so. If I had the same grace as a good man I would live as he does; but since I have not this grace, I cannot do it.' I reply that it is quite true that they have no grace, and therefore remain in their sin and cannot escape it. But this will not help them, nor does it excuse them before God, because it is their own fault. They hinder themselves so greatly and in so many ways that the light of grace cannot shine in them nor dwell in their hearts. Some of them are so obstinate that they do not desire grace or a good life, for they realize that if this were the case they would have to give up their love and desire for worldly things. And they do not wish to do this, because these things are so pleasant to them that they do not wish to forgo them. They would furthermore have to undertake works of penance, such as fasting, keeping vigils, praying and other practices which discipline the body and subdue its sinful inclinations. And they cannot do this because it appears so painful and unpleasant to them that they are frightened to think of it. As a result these cowardly and unhappy people continue in their sins.

Some would seem to desire grace, and begin to prepare themselves for it. But their wills are extraordinarily weak, for they immediately yield to any temptation that arises, although it is clearly contrary to the laws of God. They are so accustomed to giving way that resistance to sin seems impossible to them, and this imaginary difficulty gradually saps their will-power and destroys it.

Some, again, feel the influence of grace when their conscience pricks them for their evil life and prompts them to abandon it. But this suggestion is so painful and displeasing that they refuse to entertain it. They run away and forget it if they can, seeking outward distraction in creatures so as not to feel this inward pricking of conscience [. . .]

24 ━━━━━━━━━━━━━━━━━━━━━━ Chapter 16

Those who love this world are advised what to do if their souls are to be reformed before they die

Although such people are fully aware that they are not in a state of grace and are in mortal sin, they do not care; they are not sorry, nor do they give the matter a thought. They pass their time in worldly pastimes and pleasures, and the further they are from grace, the more hectic their pursuits. Perhaps some are even glad that they have no grace, so that they may, as it were, feel more free to gratify their desire for worldly pleasures, as though God were asleep and could not see them. This is one of the gravest errors, for by their perverseness they prevent the light of grace entering their souls. For the light of grace shines on all spiritual beings, ready to enter where it is welcomed, just as the sun shines on all material things wherever it is not prevented. Thus St John says in the Gospel: *Lux in tenebris lucet, et tenebrae non comprehenderunt* (John 1:5). The light of grace shines in the darkness —that is, on the hearts of men darkened by sin—but the darkness does not welcome it. In other words, these blind hearts do not receive this light of grace or profit by it. Just as a blind man is bathed in sunlight when he stands in it, but cannot see it or walk by it, similarly a soul blinded by mortal sin is bathed in this light of grace, but is none the better for it, because he is blind and does not or will not realize his blindness. The greatest obstacle to grace is a person's refusal to admit his own blindness because of pride; or if he does realize it, he ignores it and continues to enjoy himself as though all were well with him.

I urge all who are blinded and enslaved by the love of the world in this way, and those in whom the true beauty of human nature is distorted, to consider their souls and prepare them to receive grace as well as they can [. . .] And if they did so, grace would be given them. It would drive away all darkness and hardness of heart, and all weakness of will; it would give them strength to abandon the false love of the world where it leads to mortal sin. For there is no soul in this life so estranged from God by a perverse following of mortal sin that it cannot be corrected and restored by grace to purity of living if only it will humbly surrender its will to God, amend its ways, and sincerely ask his grace and forgiveness. It must accept full responsibility for its own guilty state, and not try to blame God. For Holy Scripture says: *Nolo mortem peccatoris, sed magis ut convertatur et vivat* (Ezek. 33:11). God says: I do not desire the death of a sinner, but rather that he should turn to me and live. And it is the will of our Lord that the most obstinate and misguided sinner living should be reformed to his likeness if he will but amend his life and seek for grace.

25 ═══════════════════════ Chapter 17

How reform of feeling and faith cannot be achieved all at once; it is effected by grace after a long time and with much bodily and spiritual effort

As I said previously, this reformation in faith can be achieved quite easily. Reformation in faith and feeling must follow; this is not so easily attained, and comes only after patient and prolonged effort. For all God's chosen are reformed in faith, although they may still remain in the lowest degree of charity; but reformation in feeling comes only to souls who reach a state of perfection, and it cannot be achieved all at once. A soul can reach it only through great grace and by prolonged spiritual effort, but it must first be healed of its spiritual sickness. Its bitter passions, bodily desires, and unregenerate feelings have to be burned out of the heart by the fire of desire, and new feelings of burning love and spiritual light have to be infused by grace. Then the soul begins to draw near to perfection and reformation in feeling.

The soul's progress is like that of a man who has been brought near to death by bodily illness. Although he may be given medicine which restores him and saves his life, he cannot immediately get up and go to work like a man in full health. His bodily weakness prevents this, so that he has to wait a good while, continue with his medicine, and carefully follow his doctor's instructions until his health is fully restored. Similarly in the spiritual life, although one who has been brought near to spiritual death by mortal sin can be restored to life by the medicine of the sacrament of penance, and saved from damnation, he is not at once healed of all his passions and worldly desires, nor is he capable of contemplation. He must wait a long time and take good care of himself, and he must order his life so as to recover full health of soul. However, if he takes the medicines of a good doctor and uses them regularly and with discretion, he will be restored to spiritual vitality all the sooner, and will attain reformation in feeling.

Reformation in faith is the lowest state of chosen souls, and below this level they cannot well be; but reformation in feeling is the highest state attainable by a soul in this life. But a soul cannot suddenly leap from the lowest to the highest state, any more than a man who wishes to climb a high ladder and sets his foot on the lowest rung can at the next instant fly to the top. He has to mount each rung in succession one after the other until he comes to the highest. So it is in the spiritual life. No one is suddenly endowed with all graces, but when God, the source of all grace, helps and teaches a soul, it can attain this state by sustained spiritual exercises and wisely ordered activity. For without his especial help and inner guidance no soul can reach a state of perfection.

26 ─────────────────────────── Chapter 18

One reason why comparatively few souls achieve reformation in faith and feeling

You may say that since our Lord is so good and gracious, and bestows his gifts so freely, it is surprising that so few souls come to be reformed in feeling, compared with the vast number who do not. It might seem that he is estranged from those who by faith have become his servants, or that he has no regard for them; but this is not true. I think one reason why people are so seldom reformed in feeling is that many who have been reformed in faith do not make a whole-hearted effort to grow in grace, or to lead better lives by means of earnest prayer and meditation, and by other spiritual and bodily exercises. They think it sufficient to avoid mortal sin, and continue to live in the same way. They say that it is enough for them to be saved, and they are content with the lowest place in heaven, wanting nothing higher.

It is possible that some of the elect who lead an active life in the world behave in this way, and this is not altogether surprising, because they are so busy with necessary worldly matters that they cannot devote proper attention to spiritual progress. This is a perilous condition, for they are rising and falling, up and down all day, and never attain any stability in their attempt to lead a good life. However, their way of life affords some kind of excuse. But there are others who have no need to be occupied in worldly business, and who do not have to work very hard to support themselves—for instance, religious people of both sexes who vow themselves to a state of perfection in a religious order, or layfolk who are naturally capable and intelligent. People like these could achieve a high state of grace if they set themselves to do so, and they are all the more culpable if they remain idle and make no attempt to grow in grace, or to attain the love and knowledge of God.

It is most dangerous for a soul that is reformed in faith alone to make no effort to seek God and grow in grace, nor to engage in spiritual activity. It may so easily lose ground already gained, and fall back again into mortal sin. For while the soul remains in the body it cannot stand still; it must either grow in grace or relapse into sin. It behaves like a man drawn up out of a pit, who refuses to leave the edge once he is out. He is certainly a fool, for a little gust of wind or a single incautious movement on his part will send him headlong in a worse condition than before. But if he moves right away from the edge and stands on firm ground he will be much safer, even should a great storm arise. It is similar in the spiritual life with one who has been drawn up out of the pit of sin by reformation in faith. If he thinks himself safe enough once he is no longer in mortal sin, refusing to step away, and staying as close as possible to the brink of hell, he is a fool, for at the smallest temptation of the devil or the flesh he falls into sin again. But if he leaves the pit—that is, if he makes a firm resolve to grow in grace, and makes a real effort to win it by prayer and meditation, and by other good works—then although he may undergo violent temptations, he will not easily relapse into mortal sin.

Since grace is good and brings blessing it amazes me when a person who has so little grace that he could hardly possess less, says: 'I have enough; I need no more.' But although a worldly man may have more possessions than he needs, I never hear one say, 'I have enough; I need no more.' He will always want more and more, and devote his whole mind and resources to obtaining more, because his greed is insatiable. Much more, then, should a chosen soul desire spiritual treasures which last for ever and fill the soul with blessing. The wise soul will never cease to desire grace, however much it may already possess, for whoever desires most will obtain most. Indeed, in so doing it will earn great riches and grow in grace.

27 ——————————————————————— Chapter 19

Another reason for this failure, and how an unwise reliance on outward forms of devotion sometimes hinders souls from receiving greater grace

Another reason is this. Some who are reformed in faith adopt a certain rule of life in both spiritual and worldly matters in the early days of their conversion, and imagine that they must always observe it without change, even although grace may reveal a better. They think that this rule will always be best for them, so that they love it and it becomes such a routine that, once they have fulfilled its obligations, they are quite content, and imagine that they have done great things for God. And should anything occur to interrupt their established routine, although for a reasonable cause, they are discouraged, angry, and troubled in conscience, as though they had committed a mortal sin. Those who behave in this way make it difficult for themselves to receive greater graces because they regard perfection as being dependent on certain forms of devotion, and in so doing they mistake a halfway sign for the end of the road.

Outward forms of devotion followed by people at the beginning of their conversion are good, but they are only ways and means leading to perfection, so that anyone who thinks that perfection consists in the carrying out of some bodily or spiritual observance that he learned at his conversion, who remains quite content with this, and who looks no further ahead, will largely halt his own spiritual development. In a very simple craft a mere apprentice can become proficient and understand everything as well on the first day as he will twenty years later. But in a noble and skilled craft the apprentice who makes no progress at all must be either dull-witted or perverse. But the service of God is the noblest of all crafts. It demands the greatest skill, and is the highest and hardest in which to attain perfection. It is also the most profitable and richly rewarding to one who can practise this craft rightly. So it is evident that apprentices who never acquire any knowledge of it are either dull-witted or perverse.

I am not condemning these forms of devotion used by beginners, whether inward or outward, for I know them to be good and helpful. But I would have them regarded simply as aids to spiritual development, to be used only until such time as beginners discover something better. And when the soul discovers something better and more spiritual, which withdraws it a little from the influence of the body, the senses, and the imagination, then if the earlier practices prove a hindrance, they should be abandoned as soon as this can be done without causing scandal or distress to other people, and the soul should follow the way to which it feels drawn. But if neither form of devotion interferes with the other, then whoever wishes to do so may use both. In this matter I am not alluding to devotions enjoined by the Church or by monastic rule, or to those that are imposed as a penance, but only to those undertaken voluntarily.

The prophet teaches us in the Psalms: *Etenim benedictionem dabit legislator, ibunt de virtute in virtutem, videbitur Deus deorum in Sion* (Ps. 84:7). The Lawgiver shall give his blessing; they will progress from virtue to virtue, and the God of gods will appear in Sion. Meaning that the lawgiver, that is our Lord Jesus Christ, will give his blessing, and grant his gifts of grace to chosen souls, calling on them to renounce sin, and restoring them to his likeness by good works. With the help of his grace they will progress from virtue to virtue until they come to Sion, that is, to contemplation, in which state they will see the God of gods. They will see clearly that there is but one God, and that nothing exists apart from him.

Chapter 20

How perfection can only be attained by constant effort and by purification of the desires

Now you may say that since reformation in faith alone is an elementary and precarious state from which there remains the danger of a fall, and since reformation in feeling is so high and secure a state for those who can reach it, you wish to learn the best way to attain this goal, and whether there is anything in particular which helps one to win this grace of reformation in feeling. My answer is that you are well aware that anyone who wishes to reach purity of heart and awareness of God has to fight with determination and constancy against all the capital sins. Not only must they fight pride and envy, but all the others, together with those that spring from them, as I have already explained in the first Book, because all passions and bodily desires hinder purity of heart and peace of conscience. It is also necessary to establish all virtues, not only chastity and temperance, but also patience, gentleness, charity, humility, and all others. This is not effected in one particular way but in many ways, which differ according to individual dispositions. It is sometimes fostered by prayer, meditation, and good works, while a person may sometimes prove himself by enduring hunger, thirst, cold, shame, disgrace, and other troubles for love of virtue and truth. You already know this, for you read it in every book that deals with the Christian life, and everyone who tries to fire men's souls with the love of God speaks of it. So it seems that there is no special exercise or method by which alone a soul may attain this grace. It depends chiefly on the grace of our Lord Jesus, and upon great personal efforts, all of which are little enough in themselves.

One reason for this fact may be that our Lord Jesus himself is the supreme master of this craft and the supreme healer of spiritual sickness, without whom we can do nothing. It is therefore reasonable to require that a man should follow and practise what he teaches and inspires. But a master who can only teach his pupil one lesson has little knowledge to impart, and a doctor who prescribes one medicine for all ailments has little learning. So our Lord Jesus, who is so wise and good, reveals his wisdom and goodness to his disciples in different ways, and gives to each soul the particular remedy best suited to its need. A further reason is that if there were one particular way by which a person might come to the perfect love of God, a man might imagine that he could attain it by his own efforts, in the same way that a merchant makes his profit by his own effort. But the love of God cannot be attained in this way, for one who wishes to serve God wisely and love him perfectly must desire God as his sole reward. But no creature can deserve to possess God through its own unaided efforts, for even if the physical and spiritual exertions of a single man were to equal those of all creation, he would not on that account deserve God as his reward. For God is supreme bliss and infinite goodness, and immeasurably transcends everything that mankind can merit, so that he cannot be won by any man's own efforts, like some material reward. God is free, and gives himself to whom he wills and when he wills, and not for any particular achievement or at any particular time. For though a person may do his utmost throughout his life, he can never attain the perfect love of Jesus until the Lord Jesus himself freely gives it. On the other hand, he gives this love only to those who exert themselves to the utmost, and would do even more if they could.

It seems clear, then, that neither grace alone without full support from the soul, nor a soul's individual efforts unsupported by grace, can bring it to reformation in feeling—a reformation grounded in perfect love and charity. But God's grace allied to man's effort fosters the blessed fervour of perfect love in a soul, a grace only granted in its fullness to a soul that is truly humble, and stands in awe of God. Consequently one who is not humble and zealous cannot attain this reformation in feeling, since one who is not completely humble cannot see himself as he is. For instance, he may do all the good deeds that he can, and he may fast, watch, wear a hair shirt, and practise all kinds of bodily penance; he may perform all the outward works of mercy for his neighbour, or all the inward duties of prayer, contrition, and meditation; but if he rests content with these and relies on them, regarding them so highly that he presumes on his own merits and thinks himself good, gracious, holy, and virtuous, he still lacks humility. Even though he says and thinks that all that he does is due to God's grace and not to himself, he still lacks humility, because he will not yet renounce all credit for his good deeds, nor make himself truly poor in spirit and know himself to be nothing. And until grace enables a soul to recognize its own nothingness, and, having seen the truth in Jesus, to drop all pretence of personal merit for its good actions, it is not perfectly humble.

What is humility but truthfulness? There is no real difference. For grace enables a humble soul to see that Jesus does everything, and that the soul itself does nothing but allow Jesus to work through it as he wills. But one who is guided solely by human reason and is unaware of any alternative form of guidance finds it very hard—indeed, almost impossible and unreasonable—to do good actions and then to ascribe all merit for them to Jesus and discount his own part. Nevertheless, one who has a spiritual perception of truth knows this to be wholly true and completely reasonable. Indeed, anyone having this perception will never do less good on this account, but will be spurred to a greater and more wholehearted activity both in body and soul. This may be one reason why some people strain and torture their unhappy bodies with harsh penance all their lives, and are constantly reciting prayers, psalms, and other devotions, but never come to feel the love of God in their souls, while others seem to do so in a short time and with less strain. The reason is that the former lack this humility of which I speak.

On the other hand, a person who takes no action at all cannot experience this grace. The idle man thinks to himself, 'Why should I bother? Why should I pray or meditate, watch or fast? Why should I undertake bodily penance in order to win this grace when it cannot be obtained except by the free gift of grace? I shall continue as I am, a man of the world, and I shall not adopt any of these bodily or spiritual exercises until God gives it. For if he is willing to give it, he does not require me to do anything; and however much or little I do, he will give it me. And if he does not will to give it, I shall never obtain it however hard I try.' But anyone who adopts this attitude can never be fully reformed, because he deliberately chooses worldly idleness, and renders himself incapable of receiving the gift of grace. He refuses to rouse himself either spiritually to a lasting desire and longing for Jesus, or physically to perform his exterior duties. So he cannot receive this grace.

Therefore one who has no real humility and will not bestir himself either inwardly alone, through deep fervour, lasting desire, and regular prayer and meditation, or else through both inward and outward activities, cannot be spiritually reformed to the likeness of God.

How one who wishes to reach Jerusalem, the city of peace, which represents contemplation, must have faith, be very humble, and endure troubles of body and soul

Since you wish to learn some way by which you can approach this reformation, if the Lord Jesus gives me grace I will tell you what I consider the shortest and simplest way. To explain it, I will use the simile of a good pilgrim.

A man once wished to go to Jerusalem, and since he did not know the way, he called on another man who, he hoped, knew the way, and asked him for information. This other man told him that he would not reach it without great hardship and effort. 'The way is long,' he said, 'and there is great danger from thieves and bandits, as well as many other difficulties which beset a man on this journey. Furthermore, there are many different roads which seem to lead towards it, but every day men are killed and robbed, and never reach their goal. But I can guarantee one road which will lead you to the city of Jerusalem if you will keep to it. On this road your life will be safe, but you will have to undergo robbery, violence, and great distress.'

The pilgrim replied: 'I do not mind how much hardship I have to undergo on the road, so long as my life is spared and I reach my destination. So tell me all you know, and I faithfully promise to follow your instructions.' The other answered, 'I will set you on the right road. See that you carry out my instructions. Do not allow anything that you may see, hear, or feel on the road to delay you. Do not stop for it, look at it, take pleasure in it, or fear it. Keep on your way without halting, and remember that your goal is Jerusalem; that is what you want, and nothing else. If you are robbed, beaten, insulted, and treated with contempt, do not retaliate if you value your life. Resign yourself to such injuries and disregard them, lest you suffer worse things. And if people delay you with foolish tales and lies in order to distract you and make you abandon your pilgrimage, turn a deaf ear to them and make no reply save that you wish to reach Jerusalem. And if people offer you gifts or provide opportunities for you to enrich yourself, disregard them: keep your mind constantly on Jerusalem. If you will keep to this road and do as I have said, I guarantee that you will not be killed, and that you will arrive at the place for which you long.'

Spiritually interpreted, Jerusalem is the vision of peace, and symbolizes contemplation in the perfect love of God. For contemplation is nothing other than the vision of Jesus, who is our true peace. Therefore if you really desire to attain this blessed vision of true peace and to be a true pilgrim to Jerusalem, I will set you on the right road as far as I can, although I have never been there myself. The beginning of this high road that you must travel is reformation in faith, which, as I have already said, is grounded in humility, faith, and the laws of the Church. And if you have been reformed by the sacrament of penance according to the laws of Holy Church, you can rest assured that, despite your earlier sins, you are on the right road. If you wish to make swift and substantial progress along this road, you must constantly bear in mind two things, humility and love. That is, I am nothing, and I want only one thing. Fix the true meaning of these words permanently in your subconscious mind and purpose, so that they will guide you even when you are not thinking of them. Humility says, 'I am nothing, I have nothing.' Love says, 'I desire one thing only, which is Jesus.' When deftly touched by the finger of reason, these two strings, secured by the thought of Jesus, make sweet harmony in the harp of the soul, for the lower you strike on one, the higher the sound on the other. Under the influence of humility, the less you feel that you are or possess, the greater will be your love and longing for Jesus. I am not speaking merely of the kind of humility that a soul feels at the sight of its own sin or weakness, or of the sorrows of this life, or when it sees the better lives of other Christians; for although this kind of humility is sound and wholesome, it is still of an elementary and worldly type, not pure, gentle, and perfect. I am speaking rather of the humility that a soul feels by grace as it contemplates the infinite being and wondrous goodness of Jesus. And if you cannot yet see this with the eyes of the soul, do believe in its reality. For having once caught a glimpse of his being, whether by true faith or by spiritual experience, you will see yourself not only as the most wretched of men but as worthless, even though you had never sinned. This is perfect humility, for in comparison to Jesus, who is all, you are nothing. You should also realize that you possess nothing, like a vessel that stands empty, incapable of filling itself; for however many good works you perform, spiritual or bodily, you have nothing until you feel the love of Jesus within you. It is this precious liquor alone that can fill your soul, and no other. And since this alone is so precious and noble, you must realize that whatever you may have or achieve is of no value or satisfaction without the love of Jesus. Put everything else behind you and forget it; only then can you have what is best of all.

A real pilgrim going to Jerusalem leaves his house and land, wife and children; he divests himself of all that he possesses in order to travel light and without encumbrances. Similarly, if you wish to be a spiritual pilgrim you must divest yourself of all that you possess; that is, both of good deeds and bad, and leave them all behind you. Recognize your own poverty, so that you will not place any confidence in your own work; instead, be always desiring the grace of deeper love, and seeking the spiritual presence of Jesus. If you do this, you will be setting your heart wholly on reaching Jerusalem, and on nothing else. In other words, set your heart wholly on obtaining the love of Jesus and whatever spiritual vision of himself that he is willing to grant, for it is to this end alone that you have been created and redeemed; this is your beginning and your end, your joy and your bliss. Therefore, whatever you may possess, and however fruitful your activities, regard them all as worthless without the inward certainty and experience of this love. Keep this intention constantly in mind and hold to it firmly; it will sustain you among all the perils of your pilgrimage. It will protect you from thieves and robbers—that is, from evil spirits —for although they may rob and assault you with different temptations, your life will always be safe. In short, do as I tell you, and you will escape out of all dangers and arrive speedily at the city of Jerusalem.

Now that you are on the road and know your proper destination, you must begin your journey. The departure consists entirely of spiritual—and when necessary, bodily—activity, and you must direct this activity wisely in the following way. I regard any activity that you undertake as excellent provided that it suits your particular calling and conditions of life, and that it fosters this high desire for the love of Jesus, and makes it more sincere, more comforting, and more productive of all virtues. It may be prayer, meditation, reading, or working, but so long as the activity is one which deepens the love of Jesus in your heart and will, and withdraws your thoughts and affections from worldly trivialities, it is good. But should it grow stale and lose its value, and you consider that some other activity would be more beneficial and bring greater grace with it, then adopt it and abandon the earlier one. For although the desire and longing of your heart for Jesus should be constant and unchanging, you are at liberty to vary your spiritual exercises in order to stimulate this desire, and they may well be changed when you feel that grace moves you to do so.

The relation of spiritual activities to desire is similar to that of sticks to fire. For the more sticks are laid on the fire, the greater is the fire: similarly, the more varying spiritual exercises that a man performs to stimulate his desire for God, the stronger and more ardent it will be. Therefore, if you are free and are not bound by any particular obligation, consider carefully which activity is best suited to you, and which most fosters your desire for Jesus, and undertake it. Do not deliberately bind yourself to an unchangeable routine which would prevent your heart loving Jesus freely should you receive a special visitation of grace. For I will tell you which activities are always good and essential. Any custom is good provided that it tends to foster virtue and prevent sin. Such a custom should never be abandoned, for you must always try to cultivate humility, patience, temperance, purity, and all other virtues. But any custom that prevents the adoption of a better should be abandoned as soon as time and circumstances permit. For instance, if someone is accustomed to recite a certain number of rosaries, or meditate in a certain way for a fixed time, or watch, or kneel for a set time, or observe any other outward custom, such customs should sometimes be set aside when there is reasonable cause, or if greater grace is given by other means.

30 == Chapter 22

How anyone on this road will have to fight enemies, and how he must conquer them by the knowledge of our Lord Jesus, by sacramental confession, sincere contrition, and satisfaction

You are now on the road, and you know how to proceed. But beware of enemies who will set themselves to obstruct you if they can. Nothing distresses them more than your desire and longing for the love of Jesus, and their whole purpose is to uproot this from your heart, and turn you back again to the love of earthly things. Your chief enemies are the bodily desires and foolish fears which the corruption of human nature stirs up in your heart, and which would stifle your desire for the love of God and take full possession of your heart. These are your deadliest enemies. There are also others, for evil spirits employ all their tricks to deceive you. But you have one remedy, as I told you before. Whatever they say, do not believe them; keep on your way, and desire nothing but the love of Jesus. Let your answer always be, 'I am nothing, I have nothing, I desire nothing but the love of Jesus.'

Your enemies may begin by troubling your mind with doubts, hinting that your confessions have been invalid; that some old sin lies unremembered and unconfessed in your heart; that you must give up your desire, go back to the beginning, and make a full confession. But do not believe their lies, for you have received full absolution. Rest assured that you are on the right road, and there is no need for you to ransack your conscience about the past: keep your eye on the road and your mind on Jerusalem. And if they tell you, 'You are not worthy to enjoy the love of God, so why hanker after what you cannot have and do not deserve?', carry on and take no notice of them. Reply, 'I desire the love of God not because I am worthy, but because I am unworthy; for if I had it, it would make me worthy. And since I was created to this end, although I may never enjoy it, I will still desire it, pray for it, and hope to attain it.' If your enemies see that your courage and determination to succeed is growing, they will begin to fear you.

However, so long as you are on the road they will not cease to harass you; at one time they will intimidate and threaten you, at another they will try to flatter you and seduce you, to make you abandon your purpose and turn back. 'If you persist in this desire for Jesus and continue in your first fervour, you will ruin your health or suffer from delusions and fits, as some do. Or you will beggar yourself, or suffer some injury, and no one will be willing to help you. Or the devil may put such subtle temptations in your way that you cannot resist them. For it is a dangerous course for anyone to forsake the world completely, and give himself entirely to the love of God, seeking nothing but his love, because he will encounter many perils of which he knows nothing. So turn back and forget this desire which you can never fulfil, and behave like other people in this world.'

Such are the arguments of your enemies, but do not believe them. Hold firmly to your desire and reply always that you desire to have

Jesus and to be at Jerusalem. They will realize that you are so determined that you will not yield to sin or illness, delusions, fits, doubts, temptations, hardship or poverty, life or death. You want one thing and one only, so turn a deaf ear to all their suggestions and continue regularly with your prayers and other spiritual exercises as your superior or spiritual director advises. Then your enemies will be furious, and close in on you. They will begin to rob you, beat you, and put you to all the shame they can. This occurs when all that you do, however good, is condemned and misrepresented by others. You will find that everything you wish to do to further your bodily or spiritual progress will be prevented or obstructed by others, and all your most reasonable intentions frustrated. They will engineer all these things to rouse you to anger, dislike, and ill-will towards your neighbour.

But in the case of these difficulties and all others that may arise, employ this remedy. Fix your thoughts on Jesus, and do not allow any trouble to disturb you or occupy your attention. Remember what you have learned: you are nothing, you have nothing, and loss of worldly goods is nothing, for you desire nothing but the love of Jesus. So continue both your journey to Jerusalem and your present exercises. But if, through the illwill or malice of the devil, your own frailty causes you to be harassed by the troubles that beset this mortal life, regain your peace of mind as soon as possible; stop worrying about difficulties, and continue with your work. Do not allow your enemies the advantage by brooding over your difficulties.

31 ═══════════════════════════ Chapter 23

A general remedy against the evil influences of the world, the flesh, and the devil

In due course your enemies will realize that you are unshakeable, and that you cannot be angered, depressed, or greatly affected by anything that they may do or say. When they find that you are fully resolved to face everything that may come to you, whether pleasure or pain, honour or disgrace, and that your thoughts and desires are directed to the love of God alone, they will be very crestfallen. They will then proceed to tempt you with flattery and tickle your vanity. They will remind you of your good deeds and virtues, telling you that everyone praises you and speaks of your holiness, and how they all love and honour you for your holy life. They do this to trick you into believing them, taking pleasure in this foolish conceit, and becoming self-satisfied. But if you are wise you will treat all these exaggerations as the falsehoods and flatteries of an enemy who offers you a drink of poison disguised as honey. So refuse it, and say simply that you wish to be at Jerusalem.

Such are the difficulties that you will encounter, or others like them, arising from the world, the flesh, and the devil; there are more than I can enumerate now. For so long as a man allows his mind to roam freely over a wide range of subjects, he is not aware of many difficulties. But as soon as he directs his whole mind and desire to a single objective, desiring to possess it, see it, know it, and love it—that objective being Jesus himself—he will certainly encounter many distressing obstacles. For everything that he encounters other than the object of his desire is a hindrance. I have given you some examples of this, and I add in general that any experience—whether natural or diabolic in origin, pleasant or painful, bitter or sweet, enjoyable or frightening, happy or sad—which withdraws your mind and desire from the love of Jesus to the vanities of the world, destroys the longing of your soul for him, and preoccupies your thoughts, must be disregarded, rejected, and given short shrift.

If you have some mundane duty to do for yourself or your neighbour, get it finished as soon as possible, so that it does not preoccupy your mind. If it is not essential and does not concern you, leave it alone; do not let it worry you, but put it out of mind. Say to yourself, 'I am nothing, I have nothing, I desire nothing but the love of Jesus.' Focus your mind on this desire, strengthen and maintain it by prayer and other spiritual exercises. Never let it go, and it will lead you on the right road, and preserve you in all dangers. Although you must face them they will not overwhelm you, and I am sure that your desire for the Lord Jesus will bring you to love him perfectly.

On the other hand, whatever pursuit or spiritual exercise fosters and strengthens your desire for Jesus, detaches your mind from worldly desires and concerns, and kindles a deeper, fuller love of God —whether it be prayer or meditation, silence or speech, reading or listening, seclusion or company, walking or sitting still—continue to employ it for as long as it is helpful. And as regards your food, drink, and sleep, behave sensibly, and follow the guidance of your superior as a pilgrim does. For in however great a hurry the pilgrim may be, he must eat, drink, and sleep from time to time. Do the same, for although sometimes it may delay you, at others it will help you on your way.

How a soul conformed to the likeness of Jesus desires nothing but him; and how he puts this desire in the soul, and himself desires your soul

If you wish to learn the nature of this desire, it is in fact Jesus himself. He implants this desire within you, and is himself both the desire and the object of your desire. If you could only understand this, you would see that Jesus is everything and Jesus does everything. You yourself do nothing; you simply allow him to work within your soul, accepting sincerely and gladly whatever he deigns to do in you. For although you possess the power of reason, you are nothing but an instrument in his hand. Therefore when your mind is touched by his grace and you feel yourself moved by a strong desire to please and love Jesus, you can be sure that Jesus is within you, for it is he whom you desire. Fix your eyes on him, for he does not come in bodily form but invisibly, with the hidden presence of his power. See him spiritually if you can; trust him and follow him wherever he goes, for he will guide you on the right road to Jerusalem, which is the vision of peace in contemplation. For this was the prophet's prayer to his Father in heaven: *Emitte lucem tuam et veritatem tuam: ipsa me deduxerunt, et adduxerunt in montem sanctam tuam, et in tabernacula tua* (Ps. 43:3). Father in heaven, send out your light and your truth, that is your son Jesus: and he will lead me by desire to your holy hill and to your dwelling; that is, to the experience of perfect love and to the height of contemplation.

Of this desire the prophet says: *Memoriale tuum Domine in desiderio animae. Anima mea desiderat te in nocte, sed et spiritus meus in praecordiis meis* (Isa. 26:8). Lord Jesus, the thought of you is imprinted in the desire of my soul, for my soul has desired you in the night, and my spirit has longed for you in all my meditations. And I will tell you why the prophet says that he desired God in the night, and what he means by it. You are aware that the night is an interval of time between two days; for when one day is ended, another does not follow at once, but first there comes the night and separates the days. Sometimes the night is long and sometimes short, and then comes another day. But the prophet was alluding not only to this temporal night, but to spiritual night. Understand, then, that there are two periods of day or light; the first is a false light, and the second a true. The false light is the love of this world, which is inherent in man through the corruption of his nature; the true light is the perfect love of Jesus experienced in man's soul by grace. The love of this world is a false light, because it is transitory and impermanent, and so fails to fulfil its early promise. It was this light which the devil promised to Adam when he tempted him to sin, saying: *Aperientur oculi vestri, et eritis sicut dii* (Gen. 3:5). Your eyes will be opened, and you will be like gods. In this particular he spoke the truth, for when Adam had sinned, his inward vision and spiritual light was withdrawn and his outward eyes were opened, so that he felt and saw a new light of bodily pleasure and love of the world previously unknown to him. And so he saw a new day, but it was an evil day. This was the day that Job cursed when he said: *Pereat dies in qua natus sum.* Perish the day on which I was born! It was not the day in the course of the year ordained by God that he cursed, but the day made by man, that is, the state of concupiscence and love of the world into which he was unwittingly born. It was this day and light of which he asked God that it should perish and come to nothing.

But the everlasting love of Jesus is true day and blessed light, for God is both love and light, and he is everlasting, so that one who loves him dwells in everlasting light, as St John says: *Qui diligit Deum manet in lumine* (I John 2:10). Whoever loves God dwells in light. But anyone who realizes that the love of this world is false and transitory, and therefore wishes to abandon it and seek the love of God, cannot at once experience his love, but must remain awhile in the night. He cannot pass suddenly from one light to the other, that is, from the love of this world to the perfect love of God. This night is nothing other than a complete withdrawal of the soul from earthly things by an intense desire to love, see, and know Jesus and the things of the spirit. This is a real night, for just as night is dark, hiding all created things and bringing all bodily activity to a halt, similarly one who sets himself to think of Jesus and to desire his love alone must try to withdraw his thoughts and affections from created things. In so doing his mind will be set free and his affections liberated from enslavement to anything of a nature inferior to his own. If he can do this, then it is night for him, for he is in darkness.

But this is a night pregnant with good, a glowing darkness, for it shuts out the false love of this world and ushers in the dawn of the true day. Indeed, the darker this night, the nearer the true day of the love of Jesus, for the further the soul in its longing for Jesus retires from the clamour of worldly desires and impure thoughts, the nearer it approaches to experiencing the light of his love. Indeed, it is very close. This seems to be what the prophet meant when he said: *Cum in tenebris sedeo, Dominus lux mea est* (Mic. 7:8). When I sit in darkness, the Lord is my light. That is, when my soul is withdrawn from all sinful inclinations as though asleep, then our Lord is my light, for then in his grace he draws near to show me his light. However, this light is sometimes full of pain, and sometimes pleasant and consoling. When one who is deeply contaminated by sin wishes to enter this darkness it is at first painful to him, for grace has not as yet accustomed him to it; so he tries to fix his mind and will on God as best he can, and to think of him alone. And because he finds this difficult, he is troubled. Sinful habits, with the memory of former worldly affections, interests, and doings crowd in upon him with such force that his soul is dragged back to them, and he is unable to escape their influence as quickly as he would wish. So this darkness is full of pain for him, and especially at times when he has little grace to help him. Nevertheless, if this is so in your case do not be too discouraged, and do not overstrain yourself as though you could force these thoughts out of your mind, for you cannot do it. Therefore wait for God's grace, persevere, and do not overtax yourself. If you can do so gently and without forcing them, guide the desires and powers of your soul towards Jesus. Understand that when you desire Jesus and wish to think of nothing but him, but cannot do so properly because of worldly thoughts crowding into your mind, you have in fact left the false daylight and are entering this darkness. But you will not find this darkness peaceful because it is strange to you, who are not yet enlightened and cleansed. Therefore enter it often, and by the grace of God it will gradually become easier and more peaceful. Your soul will become so free, strong, and recollected that it will have no desire to think of anything worldly, while no worldly thing will prevent it from thinking of nothing. This darkness will then bring blessing to the soul.

By 'thinking of nothing' I mean that the soul attains recollection, stability, and integrity, so that it cannot be compelled against its will to think of, or be drawn towards, any sinful, vain, or worldly thing. The soul may then be said to think of nothing, because its thoughts are not attracted to earthly things. This nothing brings a rich reward, and this night is full of great consolation to the soul that desires the love of Jesus. For it is undisturbed by any earthly thoughts, and is free to think of Jesus alone. For although the soul has banished all thoughts of the world, it is actively engaged in the contemplation of Jesus.

What, then, is the nature of this darkness? It arises solely from a grace-inspired desire to have the love of Jesus. This desire and longing for the love of God, to see him and to possess him, drives out of the heart all worldly considerations and affections. It moves the soul to recollection, and to ponder how it may come to this love; in this way it brings it into this precious nothing. But the soul is not in complete darkness and nothingness during this time, for although it conceals it from the false light it does not entirely conceal it from the true light. For Jesus, who is both love and light, is in this darkness, whether it brings pain or peace. He is at work in the soul, moving it to anguish with desire and longing for the light, but not as yet allowing it to rest in love, nor showing it his light. This state is called night and darkness, because the soul is hidden from the false light of the world, and has not yet fully enjoyed the true light, but is awaiting the blessed love of God which it desires.

If you want to know when you are in this secure darkness and when not, you may test the matter in this way, and in this only. When you feel that your will is wholly set on seeking God and thinking of him alone, ask yourself whether you wish to possess anything in this life for its own sake, or to use any creature to gratify your bodily senses. If your eye answers, 'I do not wish to see anything,' and your ear, 'I do not wish to hear anything,' and your mouth, 'I do not wish to taste anything, or to speak of earthly things.' If your nose answers, 'I do not wish to smell anything,' and your body, 'I do not wish to feel anything,' and if, lastly, your heart says, 'I do not wish to think of earthly matters, or to give my love to any creature; I wish if I can to think of and love God alone'; and when all your bodily powers respond thus— as may easily happen if you receive grace—then you have penetrated some distance into this darkness. For although unprofitable thoughts and fancies may enter your mind, and bodily desires distract you, nevertheless you remain in this blessed darkness so long as you do not allow your thoughts to dwell on them. For these foolish fancies that take your mind unawares disturb this darkness and trouble the soul, because it wishes to be free of them, but cannot. But they do not deprive this darkness of its value, for it is by this means that the soul will come to find peace in the darkness. For when the soul is released awhile from the distraction of all empty thoughts, and rests quietly in its simple desire and longing for Jesus and a spiritual glimpse of his presence, then this darkness is peaceful. And although this state of rest lasts but a short while, it brings great blessing to the soul.

33 ======================================= Chapter 25

How the desire of Jesus felt in this glowing darkness conquers every evil inclination, and enables the soul to see the spiritual light of the heavenly Jerusalem, that is, of Jesus

This darkness and night, then, springs solely from the soul's desire and longing for the love of Jesus, combined with a blind groping of the mind towards him. And since it brings so much blessing and peace to the soul, albeit of short duration, how much better and more blessed must it be to experience his love, to be bathed in his glorious and invisible light, and to see all truth. It is this light which a soul receives as night passes and day dawns. It was this night to which I think the prophet alluded when he said: *Anima mea desideravit te in nocte* (Isa. 26:9). My soul has desired thee in the night. For although the process may be painful, it is much better for the world to be hidden from view than for the soul to be out among the false pleasures of the world, which appear so attractive and desirable to those whose eyes are blind to the light of the spirit. For when you are in this darkness you are much nearer to Jerusalem than when you are living in that false light. So respond wholeheartedly to the stirrings of grace, and learn to live in this darkness. When you grow accustomed to it, you will soon find peace, and the true light of spiritual knowledge will grow within you; not all at once, but imperceptibly and little by little. As the prophet says: *Habitantibus in regione umbrae mortis, lux orta est eis* (Isa. 9:2). Light has shone upon those who dwell in the land of the shadow of death. The light of grace has risen, and will shine on those who dwell in the shadow of death, that is, in the darkness that resembles death. For just as death destroys a living body and all its powers, so the desire to love Jesus that is experienced in this darkness destroys all sins, sensual desires, and impure thoughts. And by the time this takes place you are fast nearing Jerusalem. You have not yet reached it, but you will be able to see the city in the distance before you come to it because of the twinkling rays of light shining from it. For remember that although your soul dwells in this peaceful darkness, untroubled by thoughts of the world, it is not yet at the end of its journey, for it is not yet clothed in light or wholly ablaze with the fire of love. It is fully conscious of something beyond itself which as yet it neither knows nor possesses, but it has an ardent longing for it. The object of its longing is nothing other than the vision of Jerusalem, which resembles the city that the prophet Ezekiel saw in his vision.

He describes (Ezek. 40) how he saw a city set on a hill sloping towards the south, which measured no more than a rod in length and breadth, that is, six cubits and a palm. But when he was brought into the city and looked about him, he thought it very spacious, for he saw many halls and rooms, both public and private, with gates and porches outside and in, and more buildings than I can describe many hundred cubits in length and breadth. It was extraordinary to him that this city which was so spacious within appeared so small when he stood outside. This city symbolizes the perfect love of God, set on the hill of contemplation. To a soul that has no experience of it but has a sincere desire for it, the city appears small, no longer than a rod, which is six cubits and a palm. Here six cubits represent man's struggle for perfection; the palm, a little experience of contemplation. He sees clearly that here is a reward that transcends anything that human efforts can attain, in the same way as the palm extends beyond the six cubits, but he cannot be sure what it is. But if he can enter the city of contemplation, he then sees much more than he discerned at first.

How one may recognize the false lights caused by the trickery of the devil from the true light of knowledge which comes from Jesus

Beware of the devil who walks at noon, and who makes his false light appear to come from Jerusalem. For the devil knows that our Lord Jesus shows the light of truth to those who love him, so he shows a false light in place of the true light to deceive the unwary. However, the soul can distinguish the light of truth that comes from God from that which is an illusion of the devil. I will illustrate this by an example taken from the heavens.

Sometimes there appears in the sky a ray of light that seems to be the sun itself, but is not; and sometimes the sun itself appears. The distinction between the two is this. The false sunlight appears only between two black rainclouds. Because the sun is near, a light shines from behind the clouds which looks like the sun itself, but is not. The true sun shines only when the sky is clear, or at least not overcast by black clouds. Now to apply this illustration: some people seem to forsake the love of the world and wish to attain the love of God and the light of understanding, but they are not willing to pass through this darkness that I have mentioned. They will not look at themselves honestly and humbly, and examine their former life and present sinful state, nor recognize their own nothingness before God. They make no effort to enter upon an interior life, and put aside all worldly things. They will not stamp out the sinful impulses of pride, envy, anger and such like that arise in their hearts by constantly reaching out to Jesus in prayer and meditation, silence and tears, and in other spiritual and corporal exercises as devout and holy people have done in the past. But directly they have outwardly forsaken the world—or soon after— they imagine that they are holy, and able to understand the inner meaning of the Gospels and holy scripture. And provided that they can fulfil the commandments of God literally and avoid bodily sin, they think that they love God perfectly. So at once they want to preach and instruct everyone else, under the misapprehension that they have received the grace of understanding and perfect charity by a special gift of the Holy Spirit. They are even more strongly impelled to do this when they feel themselves suddenly endowed with great knowledge after little previous effort on their part, or with what seems to be fervent love which drives them to preach truth and righteousness to their fellow-men. They regard this as a grace from God, a blessed light granted to themselves before all others. But if they examine these things carefully, they will realize that this light of knowledge and fervour does not come from the true sun, that is our Lord Jesus, but from the noonday devil who makes his spurious light resemble the sun. You can recognize this imposter by the example I have given.

This light of false knowledge shown by the devil to a soul in darkness is always seen between two black rainclouds. The higher cloud is presumption and self-conceit, while the lower is oppression and depreciation of our neighbour. So whatever appearances of knowledge and fervour may shine in a soul, if they co-exist with presumption, conceit, and disregard for our neighbour, it is not the light of grace given by the Holy Spirit, even though the knowledge may be true in itself. If it comes suddenly, it is of the devil; and if it comes after prolonged study, it is the fruit of man's own mental powers. So we can tell clearly when this false light of knowledge is not the light of the true sun.

Those whose knowledge comes from these sources are full of spiritual pride. They are so blinded by this spurious light that they regard their own conceit and disobedience to the laws of Holy Church as perfect compliance with the Gospel and laws of God. They imagine that the following of their own inclination is freedom of spirit, and as a result errors and heresies pour from them like rain from black clouds. For their preaching gives rise to controversy and quarrels, and to contentious denunciation of other people and their ways of life. Yet they claim to be moved solely by charity and zeal for righteousness. But this claim is false, for St James the Apostle says: *Ubi enim zelus et contentio, ibi inconstantia et omne opus pravum. Non est sapientia haec desursum descendens a Patri luminum, sed terrena, animalis et diabolica* (Jas. 3:16). Wherever there is envy and contention there is instability and all kinds of evil at work. Therefore the knowledge that breeds such sins does not come down from God, the Father of Light, but is earthly, bestial, and devilish. So this false light can be distinguished from the true by these by-products of pride, presumption, disobedience, anger, scandal, and other sins. For the true sun does not display himself to bestow mental light and perfect charity upon the soul unless the sky is first bright and free from clouds; that is, unless the conscience is first cleansed in this darkness by the fire of a burning desire for Jesus, which cauterizes and destroys all evil impulses of pride, vainglory, anger, envy, and other sins in the soul. As the prophet says: *Ignis ante ipsum praecedet, et inflammabit in circuitu inimicos ejus* (Ps. 97:3). Fire shall go before him; that is, the loving desire for Jesus will go before him in a man's soul, and will burn up all his enemies, that is, destroy all his sins.

For unless a soul's self-esteem is first humbled by fear, and well tried and essayed in this fire of desire and purified from all its stains by devout prayers and other spiritual exercises over a long period, it cannot endure the brilliance of spiritual light, nor can it receive the precious elixir of the perfect love of Jesus. But once it is purified and transformed by this fire, it can absorb the gracious light of spiritual knowledge and perfect love from the true sun, Jesus Christ. In this connection holy scripture says: *Vobis qui timetis Dominum orietur sol justitiae* (Mal. 4:2). The true sun of righteousness, that is our Lord Jesus, will shine upon you who fear him; that is, on humble souls who acknowledging their own weakness, esteem themselves less than their neighbours, and cast themselves down before God. They know that they themselves are nothing, and they attain perfect humility through reverent fear and constant contemplation of God.

Upon these souls the true sun will rise and illumine their minds to know truth, and will kindle their affections with burning love, so that they burn and shine. Under the influence of this heavenly sun they will burn with perfect love and shine with the knowledge of God and spiritual things, for they will then be reformed in feeling. So one who does not want to be deceived must first humble himself and hide within this darkness from all interference by other people, and try to forget the world entirely. He must follow Jesus with constant desire, seeking him in prayer and meditation. For I know that the light that succeeds this darkness is sure and true. It shines from the true sun in the city of Jerusalem to light the way for a soul struggling in darkness and calling for light, and gives it comfort in its trouble. For I do not think that a false light ever succeeds true darkness. In other words, if a man sincerely and wholeheartedly sets himself to forsake the love of the world, and by grace comes to feel and know himself as he is, and continues humbly in this realization, he will not be deceived by any errors, heresies, or delusions. For all these enter by the gate of pride, and if pride is locked out, they will find no foothold in the soul. And although they may come and seek admission, they will not be able to enter. For the grace experienced by a soul in this darkness of humility will teach it the truth, and show it that all such approaches are moves of the devil.

35 ——————————— Chapter 27

How a soul led by grace into this glowing darkness receives great benefits, and how one should prepare oneself to enter it

There are many devout souls who by grace enter this darkness and attain self-knowledge, but who do not yet fully understand this process. This ignorance tends to hinder their progress. They often feel their thoughts and affections withdrawn from earthly things, and they are brought into a state of deep peace, untroubled by unprofitable thoughts or bodily sensations. They enjoy such freedom of spirit that they can think of Jesus in peace, and offer him their prayers and psalms with great joy and sweetness for as long as the frailty of human nature will permit. They are quite certain that this experience is good, but they are not sure what it is. So I would say to all such souls that although such an experience may only be short and seldom had, it seems to be a genuine phase of this darkness which we have been discussing. For it consists firstly of self-knowledge, and then of self-transcendence through a burning desire to see Jesus; or more accurately, the experience is itself a spiritual perception of Jesus. And if they can remain in this peace, or by grace make it such a part of themselves that they can readily and freely re-possess or retain it as they will, they will never be overcome by the temptations of the devil, nor be subject to errors and heresies. They are now standing at the threshold of contemplation, able and ready to receive the perfect love of Jesus. Therefore whoever has this gift should acknowledge it with humility, preserve it with care, and cultivate it with zeal, so that nothing in existence can prevent his entry into contemplation whenever he can. Provided that he is a free agent and can do whatever he wishes without causing scandal or distress to his neighbours, he should forget and ignore everything that might prevent contemplation. For I do not think that he can readily attain this peace unless he receives great grace and submits himself entirely to its guidance. And this is just what he should do, for grace must always be free to work—free from obstacles caused by sin and worldliness, and free from all things which, although not sinful, nevertheless impede its action.

But if one who has not yet received this fullness of grace desires to attain this spiritual knowledge of Jesus, he must do his utmost to dispose himself to it, and to remove all obstacles to grace. He must learn to die to the world, and wholeheartedly renounce all love of it. First of all he must renounce pride, both worldly and spiritual, desiring neither honour nor recognition from the world, renown nor fame, position nor rank, authority nor power, worldly knowledge nor skill, estates nor riches, fine clothing nor outward display—nothing, indeed, which might cause him to be respected above other men. He must desire none of these things, and if they are given him let him accept them with fear, so that if he cannot be poor both outwardly and inwardly, he can at least be so inwardly. He should wish to be forgotten by the world, so that however rich or clever he may be, he receives no more attention than the poorest man alive.

He must not foster self-satisfaction by recalling his own good deeds or virtues, thinking that he is doing better than others because he has renounced the world while others have not done so. This makes him imagine that all is well with him. He must also subdue all feelings of anger, ill-will, and envy towards his neighbour, and avoid causing any unnecessary distress or annoyance by word or act, or giving anyone reasonable cause for anger or complaint. In this way he will be free, owing no obligation to anyone, nor anyone to him. He must also renounce greed, requiring no more than is necessary for bodily sustenance, and considering himself amply rewarded when God moves others to give him anything. He must not rely on worldly possessions, nor on the help and favour of any worldly friends. Let him put his whole trust in God, for if he does otherwise he makes himself dependent on the world, and restricts his freedom to think of God.

He must utterly abandon gluttony and all other sins of the body [. . .] He must not indulge his bodily appetites with rich food and drink, but be content with such food as is readily obtainable; for if he is healthy, any simple food will satisfy hunger and maintain the body in normal strength for the service of God. And let him not complain, argue, or be angry about his food, even though he sometimes does not get what he would like.

A man must wholly renounce these and all other sins in will, and when necessary in act, as well as anything else that prevents him giving his mind freely to Jesus. For so long as such obstacles remain, he cannot die to the world nor can he enter the darkness and attain self-knowledge. If he wishes to do so he must do all this as St Paul did, who said: *Mihi mundus crucifixus est, et ego mundo* (Gal. 6 : 14). The world is slain and crucified to me, and I to the world. Meaning that one who renounces the love of the world, its honours, riches, and all pleasures for the love of God, and who neither loves nor seeks the world, but is content to possess nothing in it—nor would if he could— is indeed dead to the world because it holds no pleasure or attraction for him. If the world passes by and ignores him, pays him no respect, and has no use for him, but forgets him as it would a dead man, then he is dead to the world. St Paul was exactly in this position, which must also be that of anyone who wishes to follow him and attain the perfect love of God, for it is impossible to live wholly to God until one first dies to the world.

This death to the world is this darkness; it is the gateway to contemplation and reformation in feeling. There is no other way. There may be many different ways leading souls to contemplation, just as there are different forms of activity to suit man of varying dispositions and ways of life, such as the religious and secular lives. But there is only one gateway to contemplation, for whatever form a man's activity takes, unless it leads him to self-knowledge and humility, and mortifies all love of the world so that he can sometimes feel himself deep in this peaceful darkness where he is hidden from the vanity of the world and can see himself as he is, then he has not yet achieved reformation in feeling, nor can he yet enter contemplation. Indeed, he is far from it. And if he tries to enter by any other gate, he is a thief and a housebreaker, who will be ejected as unworthy. But one who by grace can humble himself to nothing and die in this way is at the very door, because he is dead to the world and lives to God. Of such souls St Paul says: *Mortui enim estis, et vita vestra abscondita est cum Christo in Deo* (Col. 3:3). You are dead—that is, you who for the love of God renounce all love of the world are dead to the world—but your life is hidden from worldly men, just as the life of Christ is hidden in the Godhead from the eyes of those who love the flesh.

Our Lord himself showed us this gateway in the Gospel when he said: *Omnis qui reliquerit patrem aut matrem, fratrem aut sororem propter me, centuplum accipiet, et vitam aeternam possidebit* (Matt. 19:29). Everyone who for love of me leaves father or mother, sister or brother, or any earthly possessions, shall have a hundred-fold in this life, and afterwards the bliss of heaven. This hundred-fold that a soul will possess if it forsakes the world is nothing else than the blessing of this glowing darkness which I call the gateway to contemplation. For one who is in this darkness and is hidden by grace from worldly vanities has no desire for worldly possessions and does not look for them; he is not worried by them, is not interested in them, and does not want them, so that he is a hundred times richer than a king or other person who strives after great wealth. For one who seeks nothing but Jesus possesses a hundred-fold, for he enjoys more rest, more peace of heart, more true love and delight in his soul in a single day than the most covetous man in the world, who has all its wealth at his disposal, enjoys in his entire lifetime.

This, then, is a darkness full of blessing, a rich nothingness, which brings to the soul great spiritual freedom and tranquillity. I think that David was alluding to this night or nothingness when he said: *Ad nihilum redactus sum, et nescivi* (Ps. 73:22). I was brought to nothing, and I did not know it. That is, the grace that our Lord Jesus sent into my heart has slain and annihilated all love of the world, and I do not know how, for it was by no effort and will of my own, but by the grace of our Lord Jesus alone. Therefore I am certain that one who wishes to have the light of grace and to feel a deep love of Jesus in his soul must leave the false light of worldly love and remain in this darkness. And if at first he is afraid to live in darkness, he should not return to the love of the world, but endure it awhile and put all his hope and trust in Jesus; he will not remain long without spiritual light of some kind. The prophet exhorts: *Qui ambulavit in tenebris, et non est lumen ei, speret in Domino, et innitatur super Deum suum* (Isa. 50:10). Whoever is walking in darkness and has no light—that is, whoever wishes to hide himself from the love of the world and cannot easily feel the light of spiritual love—should not despair or turn again to the world. Let him hope in our Lord and lean on him, that is, trust in God: let him hold fast to God by desire and stand firm awhile, and he shall have light. For his condition is like that of a man who has been a long time in the sun, and then comes suddenly into a dark house. At first he is like a blind man and sees nothing, but if he waits a little he will soon be able to see about him, at first large objects, then small, and then everything that is in the house. It is the same in the spiritual world. To one who renounces the love of the world and attains self-knowledge by examination of conscience everything at first seems dark and obscure. But if he stands firm and prays earnestly, constantly directing his will to the love of Jesus, he will later be able to see many things, both great and small, of which he previously knew nothing. This seems to be what the prophet promised when he said: *Orietur in tenebris lux tua, et tenebrae tuae erunt sicut meridies. Et requiem dabit tibi Dominus Deus tuus, et implebit animam tuam splendoribus* (Isa. 58:10). Light shall spring up for you in the darkness. That is, for you who sincerely abandon the light of all worldly love and plunge yourselves mentally into this darkness there will arise the light of the blessed love and spiritual knowledge of God. 'And your darkness shall become like noonday.' That is, the darkness through which at first your desire and blind faith in God persist will turn into clear knowledge and sure love. 'And the Lord God will give you rest': that is, your bodily desires, your tormenting fears and doubts, and the evil spirits that have hitherto harassed you continually, will all weaken, and their influence will largely cease. You will be made so strong that they will not harm you, because you will be hidden from them and at peace. 'And then our Lord Jesus will fill your soul with light': that is, when you have been brought to this peace of soul you will be able to turn to God more readily, and your sole activity will be to love him. He will fill all the powers of your soul with rays of heavenly light. So do not be surprised if I call the abandonment of worldly love darkness, for the prophet called it so, saying to a soul: *intra in tenebras tuas, filia Chaldaeorum* (Isa. 47:5). Enter into your darkness, daughter of Chaldaea. That is: Soul, whose love of the world makes you a daughter of Chaldaea, leave it and enter into your darkness.

How our Lord Jesus leads a soul to be reformed by four different stages;
he calls, justifies, honours, and glorifies it

I have now told you a little about the dispositions necessary for progress towards reformation in feeling. However, I do not suggest that
you can achieve this in your own strength, for I know very well that
our Lord Jesus alone brings this to completion in whatever way he
wishes. For it is he alone who stirs a soul with his grace and brings it
first into this darkness and then into light. As the prophet says: *Sicut
tenebrae ejus, ita et lumen ejus* (Ps. 139:12). Just as the light of knowledge and the experience of spiritual love came from God, so also the
darkness which is the forsaking of worldly love comes from him. For
he does all things; he creates and re-creates. He creates by himself
alone, but gives us a share in our own recreation, for he gives us grace
and it is our willing cooperation that effects it. St Paul indeed describes the way in which he does this: *Quos Deus praescivit fieri con-
formes imaginis Filii ejus, hos vocavit: et quos magnificavit, hos et
glorificavit* (Rom. 8:29). Those whom God predestined to be conformed to the likeness of his Son he called, justified, honoured, and
glorified.

Although these words may be applied to all chosen souls that are in
the lowest degree of charity and are reformed in faith alone, they apply
more particularly to those souls that are reformed in feeling, to whom
our Lord God has given grace in abundance and showed especial
favour. For these are his own especial sons, who are fully restored to
the likeness of his Son Jesus. In these words St Paul divides God's
work in the soul into four stages. The first stage is that during which
the soul is called from worldly vanity, and this is often easy and agree-
able. For at the beginning of his conversion a person who is disposed
to receive great grace is so suddenly moved in spirit, feels such delight
in devotion, and sheds so many tears of compunction that he is inclined to think himself already half in heaven. But this pleasant stage

passes away after a time, and is succeeded by the second stage, which is that of justification. This is arduous, for when he begins to make good progress on the road of righteousness, to set his will resolutely against all sin both inward and outward, and to aspire to virtues and the love of Jesus, he encounters many obstacles, both inwardly from the perverseness and obstinacy of his own will, and outwardly from temptations of the devil. As a result he is often greatly tormented, and this is not surprising, for he has so long been twisted by the false love of the world that he cannot be straightened without great heat and pressure, just as a twisted bar cannot be straightened without being plunged into the fire and heated. Therefore our Lord Jesus, seeing what is necessary for a perverse soul, allows it to be tried by various temptations and well tested by spiritual difficulties until all the rust of impurities is burned out of it. Inward fears, doubts and perplexities will almost reduce the soul to despair. It will seem to be forsaken by God and abandoned into the hands of the devil, but it will retain a small secret trust in the goodness and mercy of God. For our Lord Jesus leaves this secret trust in such a soul, however far away he seems to go, and this keeps the soul from despair and preserves it from spiritual harm. It will also be mortified outwardly, and suffer pain in its senses. This may happen through illness, or through bodily torments caused by the devil. Or by the secret will of God the poor soul may have to suffer such pain through the wretched body that it would not know how to endure the body any longer were it not that our Lord Jesus sustains it. And yet the soul would rather endure all this pain than be blinded by the false love of this world. For this would be hell to such a soul, but the suffering of this kind of pain is nothing but purgatory; therefore the soul suffers it gladly and would not avoid it even if it could, because it is of great profit to it. Our Lord does all these things to help the soul, in order to prevent its being absorbed in worldly things and to detach it from love of the senses, so that it can receive spiritual enlightenment.

After this, when the soul has been mortified in this manner and led from love of the world into this darkness, so that it no longer takes the slightest interest or pleasure in the world, but finds it bitter as wormwood, then comes the third stage, that of honour. This is when the soul is partially reformed in feeling, and receives the gift of perfection and the grace of contemplation: it is a time of great peace. It is followed by the fourth stage, that of glorification, when a soul is fully reformed in the bliss of heaven. For there are souls who have been called from sin and justified by passing through various trials by fire and water; these are afterwards brought to honour and later to glory. For our Lord will grant all that they desired here on earth, and more. He will raise them above all other chosen souls to the glory of the cherubim and seraphim, because in this life they surpassed all others in the knowledge and love of God.

Therefore whoever wishes to attain this glory must not be afraid of this justification, for it is the only way to attain it. Through his prophet God spoke words of great comfort to all souls who are tested in the fires of tribulation: *Puer meus non timere, si transieris per ignem, flamma non nocebit te* (Isa. 43:2). My son, if you pass through the fire, do not be afraid, for the flame shall not hurt you. It will cleanse you from all the corruptions of the flesh, and enable you to receive the spiritual fire of the love of God. And, as I said earlier, this purification must be completed first, because the soul cannot otherwise be reformed in feeling.

37 ═══════════════════════════════ Chapter 29

How beginners and those who are growing in grace sometimes show greater outward signs of love than those who are perfect: but outward appearances are misleading

But you may now say, 'How can this be so?' For there are many souls now turning to God who experience many spiritual graces. Some have a deeper sorrow for sin, while others find increased devotion and fervour in prayer, and frequently receive spiritual enlightenment. Others, too, experience feelings of great warmth and sweetness. Yet these souls never really enter this peaceful darkness of which I have spoken with a fervent desire and a mind constantly absorbed in God. You may ask whether these souls are reformed in feeling or not. It seems that they are, inasmuch as they have these profound spiritual experiences which other people who are reformed only in faith do not have.

On this matter I think that these spiritual experiences, whether they consist of compunction, or devotion, or mental visions, are not the same as those given to a soul by the grace of contemplation. I do not deny that they are genuine, and are given by the grace of God. But the souls that have these experiences are not yet reformed in feeling; they have neither attained perfection nor the burning love of Jesus that may one day be theirs. But it often appears otherwise when such souls feel the love of God more strongly than those who have attained perfection, inasmuch as their emotion is much more evident outwardly, and appears in tears and prayers, prostrations, and ecstatic utterances, and in other physical signs. Indeed, to those who see them they appear to be constantly transported by love. And although I do not think that this is so, I am quite sure that these experiences, and the fervour of devotion and compunction that they feel, are gracious gifts of God given to chosen souls to detach them from the worldly love and bodily desires that have long been established in their hearts. It is only by such perceptible experiences of great fervour that these souls can be detached from these things.

However, the fervour that outwardly appears so intense does not spring solely from the intensity of their love; it also indicates the immaturity and weakness of their souls, which cannot bear God's lightest touch. Such souls are still, as it were, carnal and subservient to the flesh, and have not yet been released from it by mortification. Consequently the least touch of love and the smallest spark of spiritual light sent from heaven into such a soul is so great and comforting, so sweet and delightful, so far above all worldly pleasures that it ever enjoyed, that it is prostrated by it. Furthermore, it is so new, so sudden, and so strange that the soul is unable to endure it, but bursts out and betrays itself in tears, sobbing, and other visible signs of emotion. For when an old cask receives new wine that is working and potent, the cask swells and is nearly at bursting point until the wine has fermented and discharged all impurities. But directly the wine is pure and clear, it matures quietly and the cask remains intact. It is the same with a soul grown old in sin, for when it receives even a little of the love of God, this proves so invigorating and potent that the body would be liable to collapse were it not that God preserves it intact. Even so, the eyes break into tears and the mouth into words; but this is due to the weakness of the soul rather than to the greatness of its love. Afterwards, when all the impurities of the soul have been removed by this ferment, its love is left pure and peaceful. Then both soul and body enjoy greater peace, and the soul has much more love than before although this is less apparent outwardly. For inwardly it is now wholly at peace, and there is little outward indication of fervour. I say therefore of these souls who experience great bodily fervour that, while they have received great grace, they are not yet reformed in feeling, although they have made great progress towards it. For I consider that a man who has been deeply corrupted by sin will not be reformed in feeling unless he is first cauterized and cleansed by deep compunction. Another soul who has never been much corrupted by the love of the world, but has remained innocent of grave sins, may reach this reformation more easily and quietly, and without outward signs of great fervour.

I think the truth is that any consolation and fervour that a soul may experience in the beginning and early days of the spiritual life are as it were food sent from heaven to strengthen it in its struggle. Just as a pilgrim who travels all day without food and drink is nearly overcome by weariness, at last comes upon a good inn where he finds food and drink and is well refreshed for the time; so in the spiritual life a devout soul who wishes to renounce the love of the world and love God, and arranges his affairs accordingly, sometimes prays and labours in body and soul all day long without feeling any comfort or joy in his devotions. Then our Lord, who has pity on all his creatures, sends it spiritual food and comforts it with devotion as he sees fit lest it should perish, lose heart, or fall into depression and complaint. And when the soul experiences any spiritual comfort, and when grace has brought it successfully to the close of another day, it considers itself well rewarded for all its previous trouble and distress.

The same experience befalls other souls who are making progress and are well developed in grace. They often feel the touch of the Holy Spirit in their souls, giving them both an understanding and insight into spiritual things, and a real love for them. But they are not yet reformed in feeling, and are still imperfect. The reason is that these experiences come to them as it were unawares; they come and go before they realize, and they cannot recapture them. They do not know where to seek them nor where to find them, for they are not yet accustomed to these transient experiences. They have not yet mastered themselves by stability of mind and a constant desire for Jesus, and their spiritual eyes are not yet opened to the sight of heavenly things, although they are swiftly nearing this state. Therefore they are not yet reformed in feeling, and they do not yet possess the full gift of contemplation.

How to attain self-knowledge

A soul that desires to attain knowledge of spiritual things must first know itself, for it cannot acquire knowledge of a higher kind until it first knows itself. The soul does this when it is so recollected and detached from all earthly preoccupations and from the influence of the senses that it understands itself as it is in its own nature, taking no account of the body. So if you desire to know and see your soul as it is, do not look for it within your body as though it were hidden in your heart in the same way that the heart is hidden within the body. If you look for it in this way you will never find it. The more you search for it as for a material object, the further you are from it, for your soul is not tangible, but a living and invisible spirit. It is not hidden and enclosed in your body in the way that a lesser object is hidden and enclosed within a greater; on the contrary, it is the soul that sustains and gives life to the body, and is possessed of much greater strength and virtue.

Therefore if you desire to discover your soul, withdraw your thoughts from outward and material things, forgetting if possible your own body and its five senses, and consider the nature of a rational soul in the same way as you would consider any virtue, such as truth or humility. Similarly, consider how the soul is a living spirit, immortal and invisible, with power in itself to see and know supreme truth and to love supreme good, which is God. Once you have grasped this, you have some understanding of yourself. Do not seek this knowledge in any other way, for the more clearly and fully you can study the nature and dignity of a rational soul—what it is, and how it functions—the better you will understand yourself. It is very difficult for an untutored soul, pent in the body, to have a true knowledge of itself, or of an angel, or of God, because it pictures them all in a physical form, and expects in some way to see itself, and so God and spiritual things. But this is impossible, for all spiritual things are perceived and made known to the soul by reason, and not by imagination. And just as reason enables a soul to know that the virtue of justice requires that every man receive his due reward, it can in the same way enable the soul to understand itself.

I do not say, however, that the soul should rest content with this knowledge, but that it should employ it to seek a higher knowledge above itself, that is, of the nature of God. For your soul is a spiritual mirror in which you may see the likeness of God. First, then, find your mirror, and keep it bright and clean from the corruption of the flesh and worldly vanity. Hold it well up above the earth so that you can see it, and our Lord reflected in it. In this life all chosen souls direct their effort and intention to this end although they may not be fully conscious of it. It is for this reason, as I said earlier, that at the beginning and early stages of their spiritual life many souls enjoy great fervour and sweetness of devotion, and seem all afire with love; but this is not the perfect love or spiritual knowledge of God. You can be certain that however intense the fervour felt by a soul—even if it is so intense that the body appears unable to bear it or melts into tears— so long as its conception and experience of God is largely or wholly dependent on imagination rather than on knowledge, it has not yet attained perfect love or contemplation.

Understand, then, that the love of God has three degrees, all of which are good, but each succeeding degree is better than the other. The first degree is reached by faith alone, when no knowledge of God is conveyed by grace through the imagination or understanding. This love is common to every soul that is reformed in faith, however small a degree of charity it has attained; and it is good, for it is sufficient for salvation. The second degree of love is attained when the soul knows God by faith and Jesus in his manhood through the imagination. This love, where imagination is stimulated by grace, is better than the first, because the spiritual perceptions are awakened to contemplate our Lord's human nature. In the third degree the soul, as far as it may in this life, contemplates the Godhead united to manhood in Christ. This is the best, highest, and most perfect degree of love, and it is not attained by the soul until it is reformed in feeling. Those at the beginning and early stages of the spiritual life do not possess this degree of love, for they cannot think of Jesus or love him as God, but always think of him as a man living under earthly conditions. All their thoughts and affections are shaped by this limitation. They honour him as man, and they worship and love him principally in his human aspect, and go no further. For instance, if they have done wrong and offended against God, they think that God is angry with them as a man would be had they offended him. So they fall down as it were at the feet of our Lord with heartfelt sorrow and ask for mercy, trusting that our Lord will mercifully pardon their offence. And although this practice is commendable, it is not as spiritual as it might be. Similarly, when they wish to worship God they imagine our Lord in a bodily form aglow with wondrous light; then they proceed to honour, worship, and revere him, throwing themselves on his mercy and begging him to do with them what he wills. In the same way, when they wish to love God, they think of him, worship him, and reverence him as man, recalling the Passion of Christ or some other event in his earthly life. Nevertheless, when they do this they are deeply stirred to the love of God.

Such devotion is good and inspired by grace, but it is much inferior to the exercise of the understanding, when grace moves the soul to contemplate God in man. For there are two natures in our Lord, that of God and that of man. And as the divine nature is higher and nobler than the human, so the soul's contemplation of the Godhead in the manhood of Jesus is more exalted, more spiritual, and more valuable than the contemplation of his manhood alone, whether the soul is thinking of his manhood as passible or glorified. For the same reason the love felt by a soul when grace enables it to contemplate God in man is more exalted, more spiritual, and more valuable than the fervour of devotion aroused by the contemplation of Jesus' manhood alone, however strong the outward signs of this love. For this latter love is a natural love, and the former a spiritual love; and our Lord does not reveal himself to the imagination as he is, for the frailty of man's nature is such that the soul could not endure his glory.

Nevertheless, in order that the devotion of those souls that are incapable of such elevated contemplation of the Godhead should not be misdirected, but be comforted and strengthened by some form of interior contemplation of Jesus to forsake sin and the love of the world, God tempers the ineffable light of his divinity and cloaks it in the bodily form of Jesus' humanity. He reveals it in this way to the inward vision of the soul, and sustains it spiritually through the love of his precious manhood. This love is so potent that it destroys all love of evil in the soul, and gives it strength to endure bodily penance and other physical hardships whenever necessary for the love of Jesus. This is the way in which the Lord Jesus watches over a chosen soul and shields it from the flames of worldly love. For just as a shadow is formed by light falling on a solid object, so this spiritual shadow is cast over a devout soul by the blessed and ineffable light of God's being and the human nature united to it. Of this shadow the prophet says: *Spiritus ante faciem nostram Christus Dominus; sub umbra ejus vivemus inter gentes* (Lam. 4:20). That is, our Lord Jesus in his divine nature is a spirit that cannot be seen by us while we live in the flesh; we must therefore live under the shadow of his human nature as long as we are here. But although it is true that this love which depends upon the imagination is good, nevertheless a soul should desire to have a spiritual love and understanding of his divine nature, and all other bodily contemplations are but means of leading a soul to this. I do not say that we should separate the divine nature of Christ from the human, but that we should love Jesus both as God and man, for in him God is united to man, and man to God; but this love must be spiritual, not carnal.

Our Lord taught this lesson to Mary Magdalen, who was called to be a contemplative, when he said: *Noli me tangere, nondum enim ascendi ad Patrem meum* (John 20:17). Do not touch me, for I have not yet ascended to my Father. That is to say, Mary Magdalen had an ardent love for our Lord before his passion, but her love was more carnal than spiritual. She truly believed that he was God, but she did not love him primarily as God, for she was not capable of doing so at that time, so that she allowed all her affection and thought to dwell on him as man. And our Lord did not blame her for this at the time, but greatly commended her. But when he had risen from the dead and appeared to her, she would have honoured him with the same kind of love as she did before, had not our Lord forbidden her, saying, 'Do not touch me.' That is, Do not allow the love of your heart to dwell only on my human nature which you see with your bodily eyes, for in that form I am not yet ascended to my Father. That is, I am not equal to the Father, for in my human nature I am less than he. Do not touch me in my present state, but set your mind and love on that state in which I am equal to the Father; that is, in my divinity. Love me, know me, and worship me as God and man, and not as man only. In this way you shall touch me, for I am both God and man, and the whole reason why I am to be loved and worshipped is that I am God who took the nature of man. So adore me in your heart and give me your love as God. Let your mind worship me as Jesus, God in man, supreme truth, supreme goodness, and blessed life, for so I am. This,

I think, is what our Lord taught her, and this is what he teaches all other souls that are disposed and ready for contemplation.

Nevertheless, some people are not spiritually gifted by nature: for these and others who have not yet been refined by grace it is good for them to foster human love through the imagination in their own way until greater grace is given them. For it is not wise for a person to abandon a good thing until he can discover and use something better. The same may be said of other experiences of a physical nature, such as hearing sweet music, sensations of pleasant bodily warmth, seeing light, or enjoying sweet flavours. These are not spiritual experiences, for spiritual experiences are felt in the powers of the soul, chiefly in the understanding and will, and very little in the imagination. But such experiences are in the imagination, and therefore are not spiritual. Even when good and genuine they are only outward manifestations of the inward grace experienced in the powers of the soul. This can be clearly proved in holy scripture, where it is said: *Apparuerunt apostolis dispertitae linguae tamquam ignis, seditque supra singulos eorum Spiritus Sanctus* (Acts 2:3). The Holy Spirit appeared to the apostles on the day of Pentecost in the form of tongues of fire, and inflamed their hearts, resting upon each of them. Now it is evident that the Holy Spirit, who is the invisible God himself, was not to be identified with the tongues of fire nor the sensation of bodily heat; but he was invisibly felt in the powers of their souls, for he enlightened their understanding and kindled their affection by his blessed presence so clearly and ardently that they suddenly possessed the spiritual knowledge of truth and the perfection of love, as our Lord had promised them when he said: *Spiritus sanctus docebit vos omnem veritatem* (John 16:13). The Holy Spirit shall teach you all truth. The fire and the heat, therefore, were no more than material signs and evidences of the grace inwardly experienced. And as it was with the apostles, so it is with other souls that are visited and enlightened by the Holy Spirit, and enjoy sensible feelings of consolation as a pledge of interior grace. I do not think that this favour is granted to all perfect souls, but only to those to whom our Lord wills to give it. Other souls as yet imperfect may experience these sensations without having received the interior grace, but it is not good for them to depend overmuch on these sensations. Let them rather make use of them in so far as they help the soul to a more constant recollection of God and to a deeper love of him. For, as I have already said, these sensations may sometimes be genuine and sometimes illusory.

39 ══════════════════════ Chapter 31

The means by which a soul is reformed in feeling, and the spiritual gifts that it receives

I have now said a little about reform in faith, and have also touched briefly on the soul's progress from that stage to the higher reform in feeling. In so doing I do not intend to limit the ways in which God works to any laws of my own making, nor to imply that God works in a soul in one particular way and no other. This is not my meaning: I say only that I am sure that God does work in this way in some of his creatures. I am certain that he also works in other ways outside my own knowledge and experience. Nevertheless, whether God works in this way or in others, in several ways, over a longer or shorter period, or whether he works powerfully or peacefully in a soul, if all tends to the same end, which is the perfect love of him, then that way is good. For if God wills to give a particular soul the full grace of contemplation in a single day and without any effort of its own—as well he may —then that soul receives as much grace as it might have received after twenty years of trial and suffering, mortification, and purification. Therefore take my words in their proper sense, and as I intend them to be understood. For now, with God's help, I will speak in greater detail about reform in feeling; its nature, how it takes place, and its spiritual effects in the soul.

Firstly, however, lest you should imagine that this reformation of soul is a mere figure of speech or figment of imagination, I will support what I say by the words of St Paul: *Nolite conformari huic saeculo, sed reformamini in novitate sensus vestri* (Rom. 12:2). That is: You are reformed in faith by grace; henceforward, therefore, do not conform to the ways of the world in pride, covetousness, and other sins, but be reformed in newness of feeling. Here you can see that St Paul speaks of reform in feeling, and in another passage he explains what this new feeling consists of: *Ut impleamini in agnitione voluntatis ejus, in omni intellectu et sapientia spirituali* (Col. 1:9). We pray God that you may be filled with the knowledge of his will, with full understanding and with every kind of spiritual wisdom. This is what reform in feeling implies. For you should understand that the soul becomes aware of things in two ways: outwardly through the five bodily senses, and inwardly through the spiritual senses, which are properly the powers of the soul, memory, understanding, and will. When these powers are led by grace to a full understanding of the will and wisdom of God, the soul then attains a new level of spiritual experience. St Paul demonstrates the truth of this in another place: *Renovamini spiritu mentis vestrae, et induite novum hominem, qui secundum Deum creatus est in justitia, sanctitate, et veritate* (Eph. 4:23). Be renewed in soul; that is, be reformed, not in your outward senses, nor in your imagination, but in the higher faculties of the understanding. And put on the new man, which is re-shaped to the likeness of God in righteousness. That is, your reason, which should rightly reflect God's likeness, is to be clothed by the grace of the Holy Spirit in a new light of truth, holiness, and righteousness; it is then reformed in feeling. For when the soul attains a perfect knowledge of God, it is then reformed. St Paul says: *Exspoliantes veterem hominem cum actibus suis: induite novum, qui renovatur in agnitione Dei, secundum imaginem ejus qui creavit eum* (Col. 3:9). Put off the old man with all his doings; that is, put away from you the love of the world and all worldly behaviour, and put on the new man; that is, be renewed in the knowledge of God after the likeness of him who made you.

From these statements you can see that St Paul wishes men's souls to be reformed by the perfect knowledge of God, for this is the new experience of which he is speaking. So with his words as my authority I will deal more fully with this reformation as God gives me grace. For there are two ways of knowing God. One depends principally upon the imagination, and little upon reason; it is the degree of knowledge granted to chosen souls in the early stages of their spiritual life and progress. These souls know and love God in a human and not in a spiritual way, and think of him, as I have already said, as though he possessed human attributes. This degree of knowledge is good, and is a kind of milk which nourishes them in their spiritual infancy until they are able to come to their Father's table and receive solid food from his hand. The other way to knowledge depends principally upon reason, strengthened and illumined by the Holy Spirit. Here imagination has little place. For reason is the lady, and imagination is her maid, serving her as occasion requires. This knowledge is solid food, nourishment for souls made perfect, and it is reformation in feeling.

How God opens the eyes of the soul to perceive him, not all at once, but gradually. An example showing the three stages in a soul's reformation

When a soul has been called to abandon the love of the world, and has been corrected and tested, mortified and purified as I have described, our Lord Jesus in his goodness and mercy reforms it in feeling as he sees best. He opens the eyes of the soul to see and know him, bathing it in his own blessed light. He does not do this fully at once, but little by little as the soul becomes able to bear it. The soul does not know God as he is, for no creature in heaven or earth can do this, nor can it see him as he is, for that vision is granted only in the bliss of heaven. But it recognizes him as a changeless being, as sovereign power, sovereign truth, and sovereign goodness, and as the source of blessing, life, and eternal bliss. The soul perceives these truths and many others, but not as a bare, abstract, savourless theory, as a learned man may know him solely by the exercise of his reason. For its understanding is uplifted and illumined by the grace of the Holy Spirit to see him as he is more clearly and fully than can be expressed, with wondering reverence, ardent love, spiritual delight, and heavenly joy.

Although such an experience of God is brief and incomplete, it is so exalted and stupendous that it transports the soul and withdraws all its affections and thoughts from worldly things, so that were it possible it would wish to enjoy it for ever. On this experience and knowledge of God the soul establishes all its interior life, for henceforward it venerates God in man as truth, reveres him as power, and loves him as goodness. This experience and knowledge of Jesus, and the sacred love that springs from it, may be called the soul's reforming in faith and love of which I have been speaking. It is reform in faith because it is still obscure in comparison to the full knowledge that it will possess in heaven, for then we shall not only know that God is, but we shall see him as he is. As St John says: *Tunc videbimus eum sicuti est*

(I John 3:2). That is: We shall see him as he is. Nevertheless, this reform is also in feeling, in contrast to the blind knowledge that a soul possesses by faith alone. For as a result of this experience and grace the soul knows something of the divine nature of Jesus, but without this experience the soul believes only in the truth of his divinity.

To illustrate better what I mean, I will describe these three stages in the reform of a soul with an example. Three men are standing in sunlight: one of them is blind, the other can see but has his eyes closed, while the third has his eyes open. The blind man has no means of knowing that he is in sunlight, but believes it if a truthful person tells him so. He represents a soul reformed in faith alone, who believes what the Church teaches about God, but does not fully understand it. This degree of knowledge is sufficient for salvation.

The next man is aware of the sunlight, but does not see it clearly or fully because his eyelids obscure his vision. But he sees a glimmer of bright light through them, and he represents a soul reformed in faith and feeling, and is therefore a contemplative. For by grace he sees something of the divinity of Jesus, although not clearly or fully, because his eyelids—that is, his bodily nature—act as a curtain between him and the divine nature of Jesus, and prevent him from seeing Jesus clearly. But when he is visited by grace he can see through this curtain, and knows that Jesus is God, sovereign good, sovereign being, and source of life, and that all blessings come from him. Notwithstanding the limitations of bodily nature, the soul perceives all this by grace, and the purer and finer the soul becomes, and the less it is influenced by the body, the keener its spiritual sight and the stronger its love for the divinity of Jesus. So profound is the effect of this experience of Jesus upon the soul that, even were no other living person to believe in Jesus or love him, its own faith and love would never lessen, for its own certainty is so absolute that it cannot help but believe.

The third man, who sees the sun clearly, has no need of faith because his vision is clear. He represents a blessed soul who sees the face of Jesus openly in the bliss of heaven, unobscured by the limitations of the body or by sin. Faith is no longer required, and he is therefore fully reformed in feeling.

The soul cannot progress beyond the second stage of reforming in this life, for this is the state of perfection and the road to heaven. Nevertheless, souls who have attained this state are not all alike. For some reach this state only to a limited extent, briefly and infrequently; some remain in it longer and more frequently, and attain a higher level; while some attain a high level and remain in it for long periods when they have received abundant grace. For the soul does not know Jesus perfectly all at once, but little by little. It makes gradual progress, its knowledge of him grows, and so long as it remains in this life it may increase this knowledge and love of Jesus. Indeed, for a soul that has experienced a little of this union with Jesus, I think that nothing remains but to abandon and ignore everything else, and devote itself entirely to obtaining a clearer knowledge and a deeper love of Jesus, and in him of all the Blessed Trinity.

As I understand it, this knowledge of Jesus is the opening of heaven to the eyes of a pure soul of which the saints speak in their writings. But this opening of heaven does not imply, as some imagine, that the soul can see in imagination our Lord Jesus sitting in his majesty in a visible light as brilliant as that of a hundred suns. This is not so, for however high man's vision may penetrate, he cannot see the heaven of heavens. Indeed, the higher he aspires beyond the sun in his imagination, the lower he falls beneath it. Notwithstanding, thinking of our Lord in this way is permissible for simple souls, who know no better way of seeking him who is invisible.

41 — Chapter 33

How Jesus is heaven to the soul, and why he is called fire

What is heaven to a reasoning soul? Surely, nothing other than Jesus, our God. For if heaven is that which is above all things, then God alone is heaven to a man's soul, for he alone is superior to the nature of the soul. Therefore if grace enables a soul to perceive the divine nature of Jesus, it sees heaven itself, for it sees God.

Many people misunderstand certain sayings about God because they do not interpret them in a spiritual sense. Holy Scripture says that a soul that seeks God must lift up its eyes and seek God above itself. Some who wish to follow this injunction understand the words 'above itself' as meaning a higher or nobler level in a worldly sense, in the same way that one element or planet is regarded as superior to another. But this does not apply to spiritual matters, for the soul is superior to all material things, not because of its position in the world but because of the dignity of its nature. Similarly, God is superior to all created things, both spiritual and material, not because of his lofty place in the universe, but because of the spiritual dignity of his Being, blessed and unchanging. Therefore, anyone who desires to seek God wisely and to find him must not allow his thoughts to soar above the sun and circle the firmament, picturing the majesty of God as the light of a hundred suns. Instead, let him forget the sun and all the firmament, regarding them as inferior to himself, and think both of God and himself on a spiritual plane. If the soul can do this, it then looks beyond itself and sees heaven.

The word 'within' must be understood in the same way. It is commonly said that a soul shall see God in all things and within itself. It is true that God is in all created things, but not in the way that a kernel is hidden within the shell of a nut, or as a small object is contained within a greater. He is within all things, maintaining and preserving them in being, but he is present in a spiritual way, exercising the power of his own blessed nature and invisible purity. For just as an object that is very precious and pure is laid in a secure place, so by the same analogy the nature of God, which is supremely precious, pure, and spiritual, utterly unlike any physical nature, is hidden within all things. Anyone who desires to seek God within must therefore forget all material things, for these are exterior; he must cease to consider his own body or even his own soul, and consider the uncreated nature of God who made him, endowed him with life, upholds him, and gives him reason, memory, and love. All these gifts come to him through the power and sovereign grace of God. This must be the soul's course of action when it is touched by grace; otherwise it will be of little use to seek God within itself or in his creation.

In Holy Scripture God is described as light. St John says: *Deus lux est* (I John 1:5). God is light. This light is not to be understood as physical light, but in this way. God is light; that is, God is truth itself, since truth is spiritual light. Therefore the soul that by grace possesses the fullest knowledge of truth has the clearest vision of God. But it may be compared with physical light in this sense: for as the sun reveals itself and all material things to the eye by its own light, so God, who is also truth, reveals himself first to the understanding of the soul, and by this means bestows all the spiritual knowledge that the soul requires. For the prophet says: *Domine, in lumine tuo videbimus lumen* (Ps. 36:9). Lord, in your light we shall see all light. That is: we shall see that you are truth by the light of yourself.

In the same way, God is described as fire: *Deus noster ignis consumens est*. Our God is a consuming fire. This does not mean that God is the element of fire which heats and consumes physical objects, but that God is love and charity. For just as fire consumes all material objects that can be destroyed by it, so the love of God burns and consumes all sin out of the soul and makes it clean, as fire purifies all kinds of metal. These descriptions and all other material comparisons applied to God in holy scripture must be understood in a spiritual sense, for otherwise they are meaningless. But the reason why such words are employed to describe God is that we are so worldly in our outlook that we cannot speak of God without at first using such expressions. However, when the eyes of the soul are opened by grace, and we are enabled to catch a glimpse of God, then our souls can quite easily interpret these material descriptions in a spiritual sense.

This opening of the eyes of the soul to the knowledge of the Godhead I call reform in faith and feeling. For the soul then has some experience of what it once knew by faith alone. This is the beginning of contemplation, of which St Paul said: *Non contemplantibus nobis quae videntur, sed quae non videntur; quae enim videntur, temporalia sunt, quae autem non videntur, aeterna sunt* (II Cor. 4:18). We do not contemplate the things that are seen, but those that are not seen; for the things that are seen are temporal, but those that are not seen are eternal. It is these things that the soul should aspire to gain, partially indeed in this present life, but fully in the bliss of heaven. For the full bliss and eternal life of the rational soul consist in this vision and knowledge of God. *Haec est autem vita aeterna; ut cognoscant te unum Deum, et quem misisti, Jesum Christum* (John 17:3). Father, this is eternal life, that your chosen souls should know you, and Jesus Christ your son whom you have sent, to be the one true God.

Chapter 34

How we are to realize that it is not created love which brings the soul to the spiritual vision of God, but love uncreated, that is, God himself, who bestows this knowledge

But since the ultimate joy and end of the soul depends upon this knowledge of God, you may perhaps wonder why I said earlier that the soul should desire nothing but the love of God, yet said nothing about the nature of the soul's desire for this knowledge. My answer is that the knowledge of God brings perfect happiness to the soul, and that this happiness derives not only from the knowledge, but from the blessed love which springs from it. Nevertheless, love derives from knowledge, and not knowledge from love; consequently the happiness of the soul is said to derive chiefly from this knowledge and experience of God, to which is conjoined the love of God. And the better God is known the more he is loved. But inasmuch as the soul cannot attain this knowledge, or the love that derives from it, without God who is love, I said that you should desire love alone. For God's love alone guides the soul to this vision and knowledge; and that love is not the soul's own love for God, but the love of God for a sinful soul incapable of loving him rightly by itself. God himself is both the means by which the soul attains this knowledge, and the love that derives from it. And I will now tell you more explicitly how this comes about.

In their writings the saints say, and with truth, that there are two kinds of spiritual love. One is termed uncreated love and the other created. Uncreated love is God himself, the third person of the Trinity, that is, the Holy Spirit. He is love uncreated, as St John says: *Deus dilectio est* (I John 4:8). God is love; that is, the Holy Spirit. Created love is the love implanted and aroused in a soul by the Holy Spirit when it sees and knows truth, that is, God. This love is called created because it is brought into being by the Holy Spirit. It is not God himself, since it is created, but it is the love felt by the soul when it beholds God and is moved to love him alone. So you can see that created love is not the cause of a soul coming to the contemplation of God, for there are people who think that they can love God of their own accord with such ardour that they can merit the gift of contemplation; but this is not so. Love uncreated, that is God himself, alone can infuse this knowledge. For because of its sinfulness and human weakness a poor unhappy soul is so far from this clear knowledge of God and the blessed experience of his love that it could never attain them were it not for the infinite greatness of God's love. But because he loves us so greatly, he gives us his love, that is, the Holy Spirit. He is both the giver and the gift, and by that gift he makes us know and love him. This is the divine love which I said should be the sole object of your desire, the uncreated love that is the Holy Spirit. Indeed, a lesser gift than that of himself will not suffice to bring us to the blessed knowledge of God. We should therefore earnestly desire this gift of love, and ask God for this alone, that in his infinite love he would flood our hearts with his ineffable light, so that we may know him, and bestow his blessed love upon us, so that as he loves us, we may return his love. For as St John says: *Nos diligamus Deum, quoniam ipse prior dilexit nos* (I John 6:19). We now love God, because he has first loved us. He loved us greatly when he created us in his likeness, but he loved us yet more when he redeemed us from the power of the devil and the pains of hell by his precious blood when as man he willingly endured death for us. But he loves us most when he gives us the gift of the Holy Spirit, that is, divine love, by which we know and love him, and are assured that we are his sons, chosen for salvation. We are more indebted to him for this love than for any other love that he has ever shown us, either in our creation or our preservation. For although he had made us and redeemed us, what advantage would this have been to us had he not also saved us? Surely, none.

It appears to me that the greatest pledge of God's love given to us is this; that he gives himself to our souls in his divinity. He gave himself first in his humanity as a ransom for us when he offered himself to the heavenly Father on the altar of the Cross. This was a splendid gift, and a great pledge of love. But when he gives himself to our souls in his divinity for our salvation, and makes us know and love him, then he loves us completely, for then he gives himself to us, and he could not give us more: yet less could not satisfy us. For this reason it is said that the justification of a sinful soul through the forgiveness of its sins is ascribed and appropriated chiefly to the work of the Holy Spirit. For the Holy Spirit is love, and in the justification of a soul God shows it his love most clearly, for he takes away its sin and unites it to himself. This is the highest thing that God can do for a soul, and it is therefore appropriated to the Holy Spirit.

The creation of the soul is appropriated to the Father, because of the sovereign might and power that he displays in creating it. Its preservation is ascribed and appropriated to the Son, because of the sovereign will and wisdom that he displayed in his human nature, for he overcame the devil chiefly through wisdom and not through strength. But the justification and full salvation of the soul through the forgiveness of sins is appropriated to the third person, that is, to the Holy Spirit. For in this God most clearly displays his love for the souls of men, and it is for this that we should most love him in return. All irrational creatures, in common with ourselves, are created by God, for he made them out of nothing as he did us. This, then, is the work of his greatest power, but not of his greatest love. In the same way, salvation is offered to all rational souls, both to Jews, Moslems, and bad Christians. For Christ died for all souls, and ransomed them if they are willing to profit by his sacrifice; his death was sufficient for the salvation of all men, even though they do not avail themselves of it. And this was the work of wisdom rather than of love. But the justification and sanctification of our souls comes through the gift of the Holy Spirit, and is the work of love alone. It is not common to all men, but is a special gift to chosen souls alone. Indeed, it is the supreme work of love for us who are his chosen children.

This is the love of God that I said you should long for and desire, for this love is God the Holy Spirit himself. When we are given this uncreated love it produces all that is good in our souls, and all that makes for goodness. This love of God is ours before we love him, for it first of all cleanses us from our sins, makes us love him, strengthens our wills to resist sin, and inspires us to obtain all virtues by means of various bodily and spiritual practices. It inspires us also to forsake all love of the world, while it destroys within us all sinful impulses, carnal desires and worldly preoccupations. It protects us from the malicious temptations of the devil, and causes us to avoid useless worldly occupations and the company of worldly-minded people. The uncreated love of God does all these things when he gives himself to us. We ourselves do nothing more than allow him to act as he wills, for the most that we can do is to yield ourselves readily to the working of his grace. Yet even this readiness does not originate in us, but in him, so that all good that we do is due to him, although we do not realize this. Not only does he do this, but in his love he does even more. He opens the eyes of the soul in a wonderful way, shows it the vision of God, and reveals to it the knowledge of himself little by little as the soul is capable of bearing it. By this means he draws all the love of the soul towards himself.

The soul then begins to know him in a spiritual way, and to love him ardently. It then perceives something of the divine nature, how God is all and does all things, and how all good deeds and holy thoughts proceed from him alone. For he is sovereign power, truth, and goodness: every good deed, therefore, is done through him and by him, and to him alone are due the glory and thanks for all. For although sinful men usurp his glory here for a little while, nevertheless at the last day truth will show clearly that God did all, and that man achieved nothing by himself. Then those who have tried to usurp God's rightful place, and have not made their peace with him for their evil-doing, will be condemned to eternal death, and God will be adored and thanked for the workings of his grace by all the creatures that he has saved.

As I have already said, and will enlarge upon later, this love is nothing else but God himself, who in his love works all this in the soul of man, and reforms it in feeling to his own likeness. This love produces the fullness of all virtues in the soul, making them pure and true, tranquil and congenial, and renders them desirable and pleasant to the soul. And I will presently tell you in what way God does this. This love raises the soul from a worldly to a spiritual plane, from earthly interests to heavenly joys, and from vain concern with earthly matters to the contemplation of spiritual realities and the secrets of God.

43 ════════════ Chapter 35

How some souls, moved by grace and reason, love Jesus with fervent emotion and natural affection. And how some, inspired by the special grace of the Holy Spirit, love him more quietly with a spiritual love alone

One may say that the soul that attains the greatest love for God in this life is most pleasing to him, and because of this will enjoy the clearest vision of him in the bliss of heaven.

Love of this kind, however, cannot be attained simply by a man's own efforts, as some imagine. It is the free gift of God's grace, and is received only after great bodily and spiritual struggles. For there are lovers of God who try to compel themselves to love him, as it were by very force of will. They strain themselves by the violence of their efforts, and desire it so intensely that they break into bodily fervour as though they would draw God down from heaven to them, saying in their hearts and with their mouth, 'Ah, Lord, I love thee and I will love thee. For thy love I would suffer death.' As a result they feel great fervour and great grace. Indeed, this behaviour would appear to be good and praiseworthy, provided that it is well tempered with humility and discretion. Nevertheless, these souls do not possess the gift of love that I described, nor are they trying to obtain it. For anyone who possesses this gift as a result of grace and a personal experience of God—or one who does not possess it, but desires it—does not overstrain himself almost by physical violence in order to enjoy sensible fervour and feel love for God in this way. He realizes that he is nothing and can do nothing of himself, but is as it were inanimate and entirely dependent on the support and mercy of God. He sees that God is all and does all things, and therefore asks for nothing but the gift of his love. And since the soul realizes that his own love is nothing, he desires to have God's love, which is all-sufficient. So he prays and desires that God would touch him with his blessed light, so that he may experience something of his gracious presence, for then he would love him indeed. This is the way that the gift of love, that is, God, enters the soul.

The more fully that grace enables the soul to recognize its own nothingness in the light of God's truth—sometimes without any outward signs of fervour—and the less it is conscious of loving and knowing God, the nearer it approaches to perceiving the gift of God's love. For it is then under the control of love, which directs the soul, causing it to forget itself and be conscious only that God's love is working within it. The soul is then more passive than active, and this is the work of pure love. This is what St Paul meant when he said: *Quicumque Spiritu Dei aguntur, ii filii Dei sunt* (Rom. 8:14). All who are moulded by the Spirit of God are the sons of God. In other words, souls that are so humble and obedient to God that they do nothing of themselves, but allow the Holy Spirit to guide them and to kindle feelings of love in them by his own working, are God's children in a special sense because they are most like him.

Other souls cannot love in this way, but try to stimulate their affections and stir their imagination by meditation on God and by external discipline, so as to produce the feeling of love accompanied by bodily fervour and other outward phenomena; but these do not love God in a spiritual way. They mean well and deserve commendation, however, only in so far as they humbly recognize that their fervour is not divine love experienced by grace, but only the product of the soul's obedience to reason. Nevertheless, because the soul does all it can, the goodness of God transforms this natural aspiration to God into spiritual affection, and this is rewarded as though it had been spiritual from the beginning. Such is the great generosity of God to humble souls that he transforms these affections of human origin into the meritorious spiritual affections of his own love, as though they had come from him alone. Affections so transformed may be called aspirations of spiritual love, but they are rendered so only by the generosity of God, and are not due to the direct action of the Holy Spirit within the soul. I do not say that a soul can produce even such natural affections by itself without grace, for I am well aware that St Paul says that we cannot do or think anything good of ourselves without grace. *Non enim quod sufficientes simus cogitare aliquid nobis, quasi ex nobis; sed sufficientia nostra ex Deo est* (II Cor. 3:5). That is: We who love God do not think that we are sufficient to love or to think anything good of ourselves alone, but our sufficiency is of God. For God works in us all, both to will and to do good. As St Paul says: *Deus est qui operatur in nobis et velle et perficere pro bona voluntate* (Phil. 2:13). That is: It is God who brings about in us both the will to good and its fulfilment. But such aspirations, formed by the soul as a result of the general grace that God gives to all chosen souls, are all good. But they are not due to the special grace bestowed by the touch of God's presence in a soul that loves him perfectly. For in those whose love of God is imperfect his love works indirectly through the natural affections; but in those whose love is perfect God works directly, implanting his own spiritual affections, and destroying all worldly and natural affections. This is how God's love works directly in a soul. This divine love may be possessed incompletely in this life by a pure soul through the contemplation of God, but it is perfected in the bliss of heaven by a clear vision of the Godhead, for then all the aspirations of the soul will be entirely Godward and spiritual.

How the gift of his love is the most valuable and desirable of all God's gifts: how God, out of love alone, is the source of all good in those who love him: and how divine love makes the practice of all virtues and good works light and easy

Ask nothing of God, then, but this gift of divine love, that is, the Holy Spirit. For among all the gifts of God there is none so good and valuable, so noble or so excellent as this. For in no other gift of God save this gift of love is the giver himself the gift, so that it is the noblest and best of all. The gifts of prophecy, of working miracles, of knowledge and counsel, of enduring severe fasting and penance, and all other such are great gifts of the Holy Spirit: but they are not the Holy Spirit himself, for a reprobate soul might possess all these gifts as readily as a chosen soul.

Therefore gifts of this kind are not greatly to be desired, and they should not be over-estimated. But the gift of divine love is the Holy Spirit, God himself, and no soul can possess him and be lost, for this gift saves it from damnation; he makes it his own, and endows it with the heritage of heaven. And this love, as I said earlier, is not the natural love that is created in a soul; it is the Holy Spirit himself, love uncreated, who saves a soul. For he first gives himself to a soul before it loves him, and he creates love in the soul, and makes the soul love him for himself alone. And not only this, for by this gift the soul loves itself and all its fellow-Christians as itself for the sake of God alone. It is this gift of divine love which distinguishes the chosen souls from the reprobate. It makes true peace between God and the soul, and unites all the blessed in God. It is the bond of divine love which unites God to us, and us to God, and causes us to love one another in him.

Seek this gift of divine love above all else, as I have said, for if God of his grace will give it you, it will open and enlighten your spiritual understanding to see truth, that is, God, and spiritual things. It will kindle your affection to love him wholly and truly, and he will work within your soul entirely as he wills, so that you will contemplate him with worship and love, and understand what he is doing within you. God tells us through his prophet what we must do, saying: *Vacate, et videte quoniam ego sum Deus* (Ps. 46:10). Be still, and see that I am God. That is: you who are reformed in feeling and whose inward vision is clear to see the things of the spirit, cease from outward activity for a while and see that I am God. In other words, 'Look only at what I, Jesus, God and man, am doing; look at me, for it is I who do everything. I am love, and all that I do is done out of love. I will show you how this is true, for you can neither do nor think anything good except through me, that is, through my power, wisdom, and love, for otherwise it is not wholly good. The truth is that I, Jesus, am both might, wisdom, and holy love: you are nothing, and I am God. Recognize, therefore, that it is I who am responsible for all your good deeds, good thoughts, and holy desires, and that you do nothing of yourself. Notwithstanding, all these good deeds are called yours, not because you are primarily responsible for them, but because I make them over to you out of the love that I bear you. Therefore, since I am God and do all this for love, cease to think about yourself: look at me, and see that I am God, for I do all this.' This is something of David's meaning in the verse that I have quoted.

See, then, what divine love does within a chosen soul which he reforms in feeling to his likeness, when the understanding is partially enlightened to know Jesus and to experience his love. Love brings all the virtues into a soul, and renders them pleasing and congenial without any action by the soul itself. For the soul does not struggle painfully to acquire them as it did formerly, but obtains them easily and enjoys them peacefully through the gift of divine love alone, that is the Holy Spirit. This is supreme consolation and unspeakable joy when it suddenly discovers, without understanding how, that humility and patience, temperance and restraint, chastity and purity, brotherly love and all the other virtues that were formerly so burdensome, painful, and difficult to practise have now become attractive, pleasant, and wonderfully easy. So great is the change that the soul no longer finds any virtue exacting or difficult, but very pleasant. And all this is the work of divine love.

Others, who have the common amount of charity and have not yet grown in grace to this extent, but are guided by their own reason, struggle and strive all day against their sins in order to acquire virtues.

Like wrestlers, they are sometimes on top, and sometimes underneath. Such people are doing well. They acquire virtues through their own reason and will, but not because they love and delight in virtue, for they have to exert all their energy to overcome their natural instincts in order to possess them. Consequently they can never enjoy true peace or final victory. They will receive a great reward, but they are not yet sufficiently humble. They have not put themselves wholly into God's hands, because they do not yet see him.

But a soul that has this inward vision of God is not greatly concerned with the struggle for virtue, and does not devote itself chiefly to this. Its whole purpose is to maintain such vision of God as it has. It desires to keep its mind on this, to ensure that its love never wavers, and as far as possible to set aside all else. When it does this, God subdues all sins in the soul, overshadows it with his blessed presence, and gives it all virtues. And the soul is so comforted and sustained by the wonderful feeling of love that derives from the vision of God that no outward tribulation can disturb it. In this way divine love destroys all sin in the soul, and reforms it with a new awareness of virtues.

45 Chapter 37

How, when the soul is granted the grace of contemplation, divine love overcomes all inclinations to pride, and renders the soul perfectly humble by removing all desire for worldly honours

I will now describe more fully how divine love overcomes sin and establishes virtues in the soul. First I will speak of pride, and of its opposite virtue humility. You should understand that there are two kinds of humility, one of which is acquired by reason, while the other is the especial gift of divine love. Both spring ultimately from divine love, but the former is due to divine love acting upon the soul through reason, while the latter comes from the direct action of divine love. The first is imperfect, but the second is perfect.

The first kind of humility is born in a man when he considers his own sin and wretched condition. The consciousness of this makes him realize his own unworthiness to receive any grace or reward from

God. He thinks it more than enough that God in his mercy should grant him forgiveness for his sins. He thinks himself the worst sinner alive, and that everyone is better than himself. These considerations cause him to regard himself as the least of all men, and he struggles with all his might to resist all inclinations to pride, both worldly and spiritual. And since he despises himself, he does not assent to feelings of pride. And if he is sometimes overtaken by pride—by taking pleasure in his honours or knowledge, in praise or in any other things —directly he realizes it he despises himself and is truly sorry. So he asks God's forgiveness, humbly reveals his fault to his confessor, and accepts penance. This humility is good, but it is not perfect, for it is the degree of humility found in beginners and those who are growing in grace, and it springs from a realization of their sins. Divine love fosters this humility through reason.

A soul comes to perfect humility through the contemplation and knowledge of God. For when the Holy Spirit illumines the soul's understanding to perceive the truth, how God is all in all and does all, the soul feels such love and joy at this experience that it forgets itself and devotes itself entirely to the contemplation of God with all the love that it possesses. It is no longer concerned with its own un-worthiness or its former sins. It forgets itself, together with all its own sins and good works, as though nothing existed except God. David possessed this humility when he said: *Et substantia mea tanquam nihilum ante te* (Ps. 39:5). That is, Lord, the contemplation of your blessed uncreated substance and eternal being shows me clearly that my own substance and being are nothing in comparison to you. Similarly in relation to his neighbour, he does not judge him or consider whether he is better or worse than himself, for he regards both him-self and other men as equal, all alike as nothing in comparison to God. And this is the truth, for all goodness, whether in himself or others, comes from God alone, whom he acknowledges as all. He therefore regards all creatures, together with himself, as nothing. The prophet possessed this humility when he said: *Omnes gentes quasi non sint, sic sunt coram eo, et quasi nihilum et inane reputatae sunt ei* (Isa. 40:17). All nations are as nothing, as mere vanity before God, and are ac-counted as nothing to him. That is, compared to the eternal and changeless being of God, mankind is as nothing. For it was created out of nothing, and would return to nothing unless he who made it out of nothing maintained it in existence. This is the truth, and if grace enables the soul to see this truth, it should make it humble.

Therefore when divine love opens the inward eyes of the soul to see this truth and all its implications, the soul begins to be truly humble. As a result of this vision of God it feels and sees itself as it is, so that it gives up considering or relying on itself, and devotes itself wholly to the contemplation of God. Once it does this, the soul thinks nothing of all the pleasures and honours of the world; for worldly honour is so insignificant in comparison to the joy and love that it feels in the contemplation of God and in the knowledge of truth, that even if it were able to possess it without sin, it would have no desire to do so. Were men to honour him, praise him, favour him, or grant him high rank, it would not give him any pleasure. Neither would it please him to be a master of all the arts, of theology, or of all the crafts, or to have power to perform all kinds of miracles. He would find no more enjoyment or satisfaction in these things than in gnawing a dry stick. He would much rather forget all these things and be alone out of sight of the world, than to think of them and be honoured by all men. For the heart of the true lover of God is made so great by even a glimpse of him and a little experience of his love, that all the pleasures and joys on earth would not be sufficient to fill a corner of it. He comes to realize that these unhappy lovers of the world who are so obsessed by a craving for personal honour, and who pursue it by every means in their power, have no desire for this humility, and are in fact very far from possessing it. But one who loves God retains this humility at all times, not with weariness and struggle, but with pleasure and gladness. And this gladness is his not because he has rejected worldly honours—for that would be the false type of humility possessed by a hypocrite—but because he has received a vision and knowledge of the truth and the splendour of God through the gift of the Holy Spirit.

This worshipful contemplation and love of God fills the soul with wonderful comfort and upholds it so strongly and tenderly that it cannot find true pleasure and satisfaction in any earthly joys, and has no desire to do so. He is not concerned as to whether men blame or praise him, honour him or despise him. He is not even sufficiently moved to be glad if the scorn of men humiliates him still further, or to feel regret if they honour and praise him. He would prefer to forget both the one and the other, to think of God alone, and to gain humility in that way; for this is the surest way for any who can follow it. This was David's way, when he said: *Oculi mei semper ad Dominum, quoniam ipse evellet de laqueo pedes meos* (Ps. 25:15). My eyes are always looking to the Lord, for he will keep my feet from the snares of sin. When a man does this, he completely forsakes himself, and entrusts himself wholly to God. He is then secure, for the shield of truth which he holds protects him so well that no stirrings of pride will hurt him so long as he remains behind it. As the prophet says: *Scuto circumdabit te veritas ejus: non timebis a timore nocturno* (Ps. 91:5). Truth shall surround you as with a shield, if you set aside all else and look to God alone. For then you will not fear the terror of the night—that is, you will not fear the spirit of pride—whether it comes by night or by day. As the next verse says: *A sagitta volante in die.* Pride approaches by night to attack the soul when a person is despised and criticized by others, and is liable to fall into depression and sorrow. It comes as 'an arrow flying by day' when a person is honoured and praised by all, whether for worldly or spiritual achievements, and is liable to rest content in such transitory things. This arrow is sharp and dangerous; it flies swiftly, strikes suddenly, and deals a mortal wound. But one who loves God, seeking him constantly in devout prayer and regular meditation, is so protected by the sure shield of truth that he has no fear, for this arrow cannot penetrate his soul. If it comes at him it cannot hurt him, but glances off and passes onward. And this, I think, is the way in which a soul is made humble by the action of the Holy Spirit, that is, the gift of divine love. He opens the eyes of the soul to see and love God, and keeps them quietly and securely fastened on himself. He destroys all stirrings of pride imperceptibly and quietly, the soul knows not how, and along with truth and love he infuses the virtue of humility. Divine love does all this, but not to the same extent in all his lovers alike. For some possess this grace for short periods and to a limited extent; they possess, as it were, the beginnings of it and a little experience of it, for their consciences are not yet fully cleansed by grace. And some possess it in greater fullness, for they have a clearer vision of God, and feel more of his love. And some possess it fully, for they have the full gift of contemplation. But as I have said, one who has it even in the smallest degree has the gift of perfect humility since he possesses the gift of perfect love.

How divine love quietly destroys all stirrings of anger and envy in the soul, and restores the virtues of peace, patience, and perfect charity to its fellow-men, as it did in the apostles

Divine love works within the soul as he wills, wisely and quietly. He destroys anger, envy, despair, and all such passions, and brings the virtues of patience, gentleness, peace, and kindness into the soul. For one whose behaviour is governed solely by his own reason, it is very hard to be patient, peaceable, gentle, and charitable to his neighbours when they vex him unreasonably or do him wrong, for he is inclined to retaliate with anger or resentment, either in word, or act, or both. Nevertheless, if although he is upset and troubled, he does not over-step the bounds of reason and restrains his hands and tongue, and is ready to forgive an offence when pardon is asked, he possesses the virtue of patience. It is as yet weak and unstable, but in so far as he desires to have it, and makes a real effort to control his irrational passions in order to acquire it, and is sorry that he does not possess it as fully as he should, his patience is genuine. But to one who truly loves God it requires no great effort to endure all this, because divine love fights for him and imperceptibly destroys these feelings of anger and resentment. His spiritual union with God and the experience of his blessed love renders his soul so quiet and peaceful, so patient and devoted, that he is unaffected by the contempt and criticism, disgrace or villainy inflicted upon him by men. He is not greatly provoked by them, and refuses to be angered by them, for were he greatly provoked he would lose his peace of soul, and he does not wish to do this. It is easier for him to forget all the wrongs done to him than for another man to forgive even when pardon is asked. He would rather forget it than forgive it, for he finds this easier.

Divine love does all these things, for love opens the eyes of the soul to the vision of God, and strengthens it with the joys of love that it experiences in that vision. It brings such comfort to a man's soul that he has no cares, and is unaffected by anything that people may do or say against him. The greatest harm that he could suffer would be the loss of that spiritual vision of God, and he would suffer any harm rather than that. When a person's troubles are all external and do not affect the body—such as gossip, contempt, or material loss—he may do all this quite easily and without detriment to his spiritual life. These can be ignored. But when the body is affected and he feels pain, it affects him more deeply and becomes harder. Yet although it is difficult or impossible for the frail nature of man to endure physical suffering gladly and patiently, without bitterness, anger, or depression, it is not impossible for divine love, that is the Holy Spirit, to bring this about in a soul when he grants it the precious gift of himself. To one in distress he grants the mighty experience of his love, and unites it to himself in a wonderful manner. By his great power he withdraws it from the influence of the outward senses, and bestows such sweet comfort on the soul by his sacred presence that it is aware of little or no bodily pain. This is an especial grace granted to the holy martyrs and apostles, of whom holy scripture says: *Ibant Apostoli gaudentes a conspectu concilii, quoniam digni habiti sunt pro nomine Christi contumeliam pati* (Acts 5:41). The apostles came joyfully from the Council of the Jews when they were beaten with scourges, and they were glad to be held worthy to suffer bodily distress for the love of Jesus. They were not moved to anger and resentment, and had no wish to be revenged on the Jews who beat them, as a worldly man would be when he suffers even a small wrong from his neighbours. Nor were they stirred to pride and self-conceit so as to despise and condemn the Jews, as happens with hypocrites and heretics who will endure great bodily pain and are sometimes ready to suffer death with great joy and strength of purpose, as though in the name of Jesus and for love of him. In fact this love and joy that they feel in bodily suffering is not to be identified with that implanted by the Holy Spirit [. . .] But when one who loves God suffers hurt from his neighbours, he is so strengthened by the grace of the Holy Spirit, and made so humble, patient, and peaceable, that he always maintains his humility whatever wrong he may suffer. He does not despise or denounce one who injures him, but prays for him in his heart, and has a deeper pity and compassion for him than for others who have never harmed him. Indeed, he loves him more, and desires his salvation more fervently because he knows that he himself will reap a great spiritual reward from the other's unkindness, although this was not his intention. But love and humility of this degree are beyond unaided human attainment; they become possible only by the working of the Holy Spirit in those whom he makes true lovers of God.

47 ══════════════════════ Chapter 39

How divine love destroys covetousness, impurity, and gluttony, together with all enjoyment of sensual pleasures, doing so quietly and easily through the grace of contemplation

Covetousness is destroyed in the soul by the working of divine love, for it stirs the soul to such an ardent desire for good and heavenly riches that it holds all earthly riches as worthless. It sets no greater value on a precious stone than on a lump of chalk, and is no more attracted by a hundred pounds of gold than by a pound of lead. It knows that all perishable things are of equal value, and does not esteem one more highly than another, since it is fully aware that all these earthly things that worldly men regard so highly and love so greatly will pass away and come to nothing, both the things themselves and the love which they inspire. Therefore in his mind such a person already sees these things as they will be hereafter, and accounts them as nothing. And while those who love this world struggle and intrigue for earthly goods, one against the other, the man who loves God strives against nobody. He possesses his soul in peace, and remains content with what he has, refusing to seek anything more. He wants no greater share of all the world's riches than will provide for his bare bodily needs for as long as God wills him to live. This he can easily obtain, and desires no more. He is well content when his bare needs are satisfied for the time being, so that he is spared the necessity of maintaining and administering property, and can devote his whole heart and energy to seeking God and finding him in purity of spirit. And since only the 'pure in heart shall see God', this is his sole desire. Consequently the love of father, mother, and friends does not influence him unduly, for the sword of spiritual love severs all earthly love from his heart, so that he feels no deeper affection towards his father, mother, and friends than towards other people unless he sees greater virtue or grace in them than in others. On the other hand, he would prefer to see the same grace in his own father and mother than he sees in certain others; but if this is not so, then he loves others who possess more. And this is true charity. Thus divine love destroys worldly covetousness, and brings poverty of spirit into the soul.

Divine love effects this transformation not only in those who have no worldly possessions, but also in some who enjoy high rank and have great riches at their disposal. Love overcomes covetousness in some of these to such a degree that they value their riches no more than a straw. And if those who are entrusted with their care lose them by negligence, they take no account of it. The reason for this is that the heart of one who loves God is by the gift of the Holy Spirit so fully occupied with the consideration and love of that which is supremely precious and valuable that it finds no satisfaction in any other love that conflicts with this.

Divine love also destroys inclinations to lust and bodily impurity, introduces true chastity into the soul, and causes it to love it. For the soul feels such joy at the vision of God that it takes pleasure in being chaste, and finds no difficulty in preserving chastity, for by so doing it is most at ease and most at peace.

In the same manner Divine love uproots gluttony, and makes a man sober and temperate. It gives him such support that he has no craving for food and drink, but takes whatever best meets his needs if it is readily available. He does so not out of love for self, but love of God. One who loves God is well aware that he must sustain his bodily life with food and drink for as long as God wills. Therefore one in whom the love of God dwells must, I think, exercise discretion and take such bodily sustenance as will best enable him to preserve this grace and present fewest obstacles to its working within him. If possible, he will choose the kind of food that is least troublesome and maintains his bodily strength, whether meat and fish, or only bread and ale. For the whole purpose of such a man is to keep his mind fixed constantly on God, and, if possible, to do this without interruption. But since this is bound to suffer interruption at times, the less that food and drink intervene, the better it is. He would rather make use of the best and most costly of food if this interfered less with the custody of his heart, than to take only bread and water if it involved more disturbance, for he is not concerned to acquire great merit by fasting if this causes him to lose his peace of heart. His whole purpose is to keep his heart as steadfastly as possible in the sight of God and in the experience of his love. In fact, I think he might eat the richest fare with less pleasure than another man who, guided solely by reason and without this special gift of love, might eat the poorest fare. Rich dishes prepared solely to tempt the palate are not proper food for such a man; on the other hand, if simple food, such as bread and ale, help him best and keep his heart at peace, it will be best for him to use them, especially if his physical strength is sustained by the gift of divine love.

Yet divine love does even more than this. It cures spiritual inertia and bodily idleness, and makes the soul zealous and eager for the service of God. Indeed, it desires to be constantly occupied in godly activity, that is, in the contemplation of God. Through this the soul finds joy and delight in prayer and meditation, and in the doing of all else that requires to be done without reluctance and bitterness, whether the person be a religious or a layman.

Divine love also checks any foolish tendency to pamper the bodily senses. It controls the sense of sight, so that a person takes no pleasure in seeing worldly things; on the contrary, they disturb him, however beautiful, precious, or wonderful they may be. Those who love the world rush off to see new things, to wonder at them, and to satisfy their hearts with unprofitable gazing at them. But one who loves God tries to withdraw and avoid the sight of such things, so that his spiritual vision may not be impaired. For in the spirit he sees what is far more beautiful, and he has no desire to lose this.

The same applies to speech and hearing. It is painful to the soul of one who loves God to discuss or listen to anything that might lessen his freedom to think of God alone. Any song or music that impairs his ability to pray or meditate upon God freely and peacefully is repugnant to him, and the more delightful it is to other people, the more distasteful it is to him. Similarly, to hear others speaking, unless it furthers the progress of his soul in the love of God, is of no pleasure to him. Indeed, it soon becomes irksome to him. He would rather be at peace, hearing nothing and saying nothing, than listen to the greatest scholar on earth advancing all the arguments known to the mind of man unless he were able to speak with sincerity and fervour of the love of God. For this is his own principal occupation, and he has no wish to discuss, hear, or see anything but what may help him and lead him to a deeper knowledge and closer experience of God. So he certainly has no desire to discuss or listen to worldly matters, nor has he any interest in worldly stories, news, or empty gossip of any kind.

It is the same with the senses of smell, taste, and touch; the more that his thoughts are distracted and his peace of soul disturbed by the sense of smell, taste, or any other physical sense, the more he avoids it. The less he is aware of them the better he is pleased, and were it possible to live in the body without being aware of any of them, he would gladly do so. For they often trouble the heart and disturb its peace, and they cannot be entirely avoided. Nevertheless, the love of God is sometimes so powerful in a soul that it overcomes and uproots all that obstructs it.

48 ———————————— Chapter 40

On the virtues and graces which a soul receives when its spiritual eyes are opened and it is given the grace of contemplation. How these cannot be won by its own unaided efforts, but only with the assistance of especial grace

These are the ways through which divine love works in a soul, opening its spiritual eyes to see God by the infusion of an especial grace, and rendering it pure, refined, and capable of contemplation. Even the greatest theologian on earth could not conceive of or define the real nature of this opening of the spiritual eyes. For it cannot be attained by study, or by a person's own unaided efforts. It is made possible principally by the grace of the Holy Spirit; a person's own efforts are only secondary. I am reluctant to speak of it at all, for I do not think that I am capable of doing so. It is beyond my capacity, and my lips are not pure. However, since divine love seems to ask and demand it of me, I will attempt to say a little more on the matter, trusting in its guidance. This opening of the spiritual eyes is that glowing darkness and rich nothingness of which I spoke earlier. It may be called: *Purity of soul and spiritual rest, inward stillness and peace of conscience, refinement of thought and integrity of soul, a lively consciousness of grace and solitude of heart, the wakeful sleep of the spouse and the tasting of heavenly joys, the ardour of love and brightness of light, the entry into contemplation and reformation in feeling.* All these terms are employed by various writers in spiritual literature, for each of them spoke from his own experience of grace; and although they use different expressions, they are all speaking of the same truth.

If a soul through grace has any one of these experiences, it has all, for when a soul longs to see the face of God, and is touched by the especial grace of the Holy Spirit, it is suddenly changed and uplifted from its former condition to a different level of experience. First of all, it is detached in a wonderful way from the love and desire for all earthly things and withdrawn into itself. And so great is this change that it has lost all desire for worldly things, and for everything save God alone. Then it is *cleansed from all the foulness of sin*. This cleansing is so complete that the memory of sin and all inordinate affection for any created thing is suddenly washed away and expunged, and nothing remains to separate the soul from God but the limitations of bodily existence. Then it is *in spiritual rest*, for all painful doubts and fears, and all other temptations of its spiritual enemies, are driven from the heart, so that they cease to trouble or vex it during this time. It is at rest from the pressure of worldly affairs and the troublesome assaults of sinful inclinations, but is free to engage in the activity of love. And the greater its activity in love, the more complete its rest.

This restful activity is very different to physical idleness and blind security. It is a state of intense spiritual activity, but it is called restful because grace removes the heavy burden of worldly love from the soul, and makes it strong and free through the gift of the Holy Spirit of love, so that it can undertake everything to which grace inspires it, with joy, ease, and delight. It is called a holy inactivity and a most active rest—and so it is—because the soul is *in stillness* from the horrid din of carnal desires and impure thoughts.

This stillness is brought about by the Holy Spirit in the contemplation of God, for his voice is so sweet and so powerful that it silences the clamour of all other voices in the soul. It is a mighty voice, sounding gently in a pure soul, of which the prophet says: *Vox Domini in virtute* (Ps. 29:4). The voice of the Lord is a mighty voice. The word of this voice is living and powerful, as the apostle says: *Vivus est sermo Domini et efficax, penetrabilior omni gladio* (Heb. 4:12). The word of God is living and powerful, and sharper than any sword. Fleshly love is slain at the sound of his word, and the soul is guarded in silence from all sinful inclinations. The Apocalypse says of this silence: *Factum est silentium in caelo, quasi media hora* (Rev. 8:1). There was silence in heaven about the space of half an hour. Heaven represents a pure soul raised by grace from earthly love to converse with heaven; such a soul is in silence. But since that silence cannot remain unbroken for ever because of the corruption of human nature, it is compared to an interval of half an hour. However long this interval may be, it appears short to the soul, and is therefore represented by half an hour. The soul meanwhile enjoys *peace of conscience*, for grace banishes the pain and remorse, the restlessness and strain caused by sin, and brings peace and reconciliation, uniting God and the soul in a single will. There is no harsh reproof of the soul for its sins and failures, for God and the soul have kissed and are friends. All its misdoings have been forgiven.

The soul now feels humble security and great joy, and this reconciliation gives it full assurance of salvation, for the Holy Spirit witnesses to its inmost conscience that it is a son chosen to receive his heritage in heaven. As St Paul says: *Ipse Spiritus testimonium perhibet spiritui nostro, quod filii Dei sumus* (Rom. 8:16). The Holy Spirit bears witness to our spirit that we are the sons of God. This testimony which grace affords to our conscience is the true joy of the soul, as the apostle says: *Gloria mea est testimonium conscientiae meae* (II Cor. 1:12). My joy is witness to my conscience; that is, the joy that I feel bears witness to the peace and reconciliation, the true love and friendship between God and my soul. And when the soul is in this state of peace, it is also *refined in thought*.

When the soul is enslaved by love of the world, it falls lower than all other creatures, for all things hold it in their power and overmaster it, so that it cannot see or love God. For just as the love of the world is unprofitable and materialistic, so also the love and reliance on creatures is materialistic, and reduces the soul to slavery. But when the eyes of the soul are opened to see God, this love is transfigured and the soul exalted to its own proper nature above all material things. It then considers and employs them in a spiritual way, for its love is spiritual. The soul will therefore utterly refuse to make itself the slave of material loves, for grace has raised it high above them. It sets no value on the world, because it will soon pass away and perish. While the soul is maintained in this exaltation of heart, no error or trick of the devil can influence it, for its gaze is fixed so closely on God that all things are beneath it. The prophet speaks of this state, saying: *Accedat homo ad cor altum; et exaltabitur Deus* (Ps. 64:6). Let man come to exaltation of heart, and God himself shall be glorified. That is, a man who by grace comes to be exalted in thought shall see that

God alone is exalted above all creatures, and that the soul itself is exalted in him.

The soul is then alone, for it is entirely estranged from the society of those who love the world, although it still remains among them bodily. It has entirely renounced all worldly love of creatures, and is not concerned if it never sees or speaks to a man, or receives comfort from one, so long as it may always continue in the same spiritual state. For it is so deeply conscious of the intimate and blessed presence of God, and so delights in him, that for his love it can easily forgo all love of worldly creatures and even abandon the memory of them. I do not say that it will no longer love or think of other creatures, but rather that it will think of them at the right times, and will regard them and love them with a free and spiritual love, not with an anxious and carnal love as heretofore. The prophet speaks of this spiritual solitude, saying: *Ducam eam in solitudinem, et loquar ad cor ejus* (Hos. 2:14). I will lead her into the wilderness, and speak to her heart. That is, the grace of God leads a soul from the distasteful company of carnal desires into solitude of mind, causes it to forget the pleasures of the world, and by its sweet influence breathes words of love into its heart. A soul is truly solitary when it loves God and devotes itself wholly to him, and has lost all taste for the consolations of the world. And the better to maintain this solitude, it retires from the company of men if it can, and seeks physical solitude, since this greatly promotes solitude of soul and the free working of divine love. And the less interference it suffers from empty chatter without or unprofitable thoughts within, the freer it is to contemplate God. In this way it attains *solitude of heart*.

While a soul is obsessed and blinded by love of the world, it is entirely earth-bound, and like a highway, is common ground for everything, because every impulse of the flesh or the devil enters and passes through it. Then grace draws it into an inner chamber and into the presence of God, where it hears his secret counsels and is wonderfully comforted by them. Of this the prophet says: *Secretum meum mihi; secretum meum mihi* (Isa. 24:16). My secret is my own, my secret is my own. That is, one who loves God, whom grace has raised from the outward feelings of worldly love and caught up into the secrets of spiritual love, gives thanks to him, saying: My secret is my own. Meaning, O Lord my God, your secret is revealed to me and hidden from all lovers of the world, for it is called hidden manna, whose nature can be more easily enquired about than defined. And

God makes this promise to one who loves him: *Dabo ei manna absconditum, quod nemo novit, nisi qui accipit* (Rev. 2:17). This manna is heavenly food and the bread of angels, as Holy Scripture says. For angels are fed and filled by the clear sight and burning love of God; and that is manna. For we may ask what it is, but we cannot fully understand. One who loves God is not filled with manna here, but while he remains in the body he receives a small taste of it.

This tasting of manna is a lively consciousness of grace, which is due to the quickening of the soul's spiritual vision. This grace is no different from that experienced by a chosen soul at the beginning of its conversion; it is the self-same grace experienced and revealed in a different way, for grace increases with the soul, and the soul with grace. And the purer the soul and the more withdrawn from love of the world, the more powerful is grace, and the more inward and spiritual is the soul's experience of the presence of God. So the same grace which first turns a man from sin and enables him to begin and make progress by the exercise of virtues and good works, also makes him perfect. And this form of grace is called a *lively consciousness of grace*, for one who possesses it feels it strongly, and is fully conscious by experience that he is in grace. To him it is lively indeed, for it wonderfully refreshes the soul, and infuses such health into it that it does not feel the pain of bodily disease, although the body may be feeble and sickly. For the power of grace is such that both body and soul are brought to their fullest health and ease.

When this grace is withdrawn, the soul is plunged into sorrow, for it thinks that it will be able to retain it always, and that nothing can take it away. But this is not so, for it passes away very easily. Nevertheless, although the consciousness of grace in all its fullness passes away, its influence remains; it preserves the soul in tranquillity, and makes it desire the return of grace. This is also what is known as the *wakeful sleep of the spouse* of which Holy Scripture says: *Ego dormio, et cor meum vigilat* (S. of S. 5:2). I sleep, and my heart keeps watch. That is: I am spiritually at rest, when the love of the world is destroyed within me by grace, and the sinful impulses of bodily desires are so deadened that I hardly feel them and they do not trouble me. My heart is set free, and then it keeps watch, for it is vigilant and ready to love and see God. The more deeply I am at rest from outward things, the more awake I am to the knowledge of God and of inward things. I cannot be awake to Jesus unless I am asleep to the world. So while the grace of God closes the bodily eyes, the soul is asleep to the vanities of the world: the eyes of the spirit are opened, and it wakes to the sight of God's majesty hidden within the clouds of his precious humanity. As the Gospel says of the apostles when they were with the Lord Jesus at his transfiguration, they first slept, and then *vigilantes viderunt majestatem* (Luke 9:32); they woke to see his majesty. This sleep of the apostles represents the soul's death to worldly love through the inspiration of the Holy Spirit, and their awakening represents its contemplation of God. Through this sleep the soul is brought from the turmoil of worldly desires into peace, and through this awakening it is raised up to the sight of God and spiritual things. The closer that the eyes of the soul are shut to earthly things in this kind of sleep, the keener is its inward vision, which is enabled to see the beauty of heaven in loving contemplation. This sleep and this awakening are wrought by the light of grace in the soul of one who loves God.

49 ══════════════════════ Chapter 41

How the special grace of the contemplation of God is sometimes withdrawn from a soul; how a soul should act in the absence or presence of God; and how a soul should constantly desire the gracious presence of God

Show me a soul whose eyes have been opened by the action of grace to the contemplation of God, a soul so entirely detached and with-drawn from love of the world that it possesses *purity and poverty of spirit, spiritual rest, inward stillness and peace of conscience, refinement of thought, solitude and retirement of heart, and the wakeful sleep of the spouse.* Show me a soul that has lost all desire and love for the world, that is enraptured by the joys of heaven, and continually athirst for and quietly seeking the blessed presence of God. Then I can say with full conviction that this soul is burning with love and radiant with spiritual light. It is worthy to be called the spouse of Christ, for it is reformed in feeling, and ready to receive the grace of contemplation. These are the signs of the inspiration which comes to it when the eyes of the soul are opened, for when its eyes are opened the soul has for the time being the full exercise of all these gifts that I have mentioned.

Nevertheless, it often happens that grace is partly withdrawn because of the weakness and corruption of human nature, and the soul relapses into its former subjection to the body. This causes it great sorrow and pain, for it is blind, insensate, and incapable of good. It is weak and powerless, burdened with the body and the bodily senses. And when the soul seeks and desires the grace of God again, it cannot find it. For Holy Scripture says of God: *Postquam vultum suum absconderit, non est qui contempletur eum* (Job 34:29). When God has hidden his face, none may behold him. When God reveals himself, the soul cannot help but see him, for he is light; and when he hides himself, it cannot see him because it is in darkness. God's hiding of himself is only a subtle testing of the soul, and his revealing of himself is to comfort the soul by his wondrous goodness and mercy.

Do not be surprised when all consciousness of grace is sometimes withdrawn from one who loves God. For holy scripture says that the spouse shares the same lot: *Quaesivi et non inveni illum: vocavi et non respondit mihi* (S. of S. 3:1). I sought him, and did not find him; I called, but he did not answer. That is; when I relapse into my natural weakness, grace is withdrawn, and the cause of this is my own failure, and not his departure from me. But when God is absent from me I am miserable, so I seek him with great and heartfelt desire; but he gives me no answer that I can hear. Then I cry with all my soul: *Revertere, dilecte, mihi!* (S. of S. 2:17). Return to me, my beloved! But even then he does not seem to have heard me. The painful consciousness of myself, the assaults of worldly loves and fears, together with my own lack of spiritual strength, unite in a continual cry from my soul to God. Even so, God remains withdrawn for a while and does not come, however constant my cry. He acts thus because he is sure of one who loves him, and knows that he will not entirely relapse into love of the world, because he no longer has any desire for it. So God remains withdrawn from the soul the longer.

But at last, when he wills, God returns, full of grace and truth, and visits the soul which is fainting with desire and seeking his presence with so much love. He gently touches it, anoints it with the oil of gladness, and relieves all its pain. Then the soul cries out to God with heartfelt gladness: *Oleum effusum nomen tuum* (S. of S. 1:2). Your name, O God, is like oil poured out. For as long as my soul is sick and sore with sin, burdened by the body, saddened and disquieted by the perils and miseries of this life so long, O Lord God, your name to me is not oil poured out, but sealed up. But when my soul is suddenly flooded with the light of grace, soothed and healed from all the filth of sin, and when divine light and love brings spiritual strength and unspeakable joy, then I can say with hearty praise and gladness of spirit: 'Your name, O Lord, is oil poured out to me.' For by your gracious visitation the true significance of your name is revealed to me, that you are JESUS, healing. For your gracious presence alone can raise me from sorrow and from sin.

Blessed is the soul that is constantly fed by the experience of God's love when he is present, and supported by the desire for him when he is absent. Wise and well grounded is the lover of God who behaves himself humbly and reverently in his presence, who contemplates him with love but without familiarity, and who remains patient and calm, without despair and bitterness, when he is absent.

This variable feeling of the absence and presence of God does not mean that the soul has attained perfection, nor does it prevent the soul receiving the grace of perfection or of contemplation; but in so far as it persists, the soul remains less than perfect. For the more a soul hinders itself from reaching a continual awareness of grace, the less grace it enjoys. However, the grace that it already possesses is the grace of contemplation. For this variable feeling of the absence and presence of God occurs in the state of perfection, as well as in the beginning of the spiritual life, but in a different way. And just as the presence of grace is experienced in different ways in these two states, so is the absence of grace. As a result, one who does not realize when grace is absent is liable to be deceived, and one who does not recognize the presence of grace will not be grateful when it comes to him, whether he is a beginner or has entered the state of perfection. Nevertheless, the more stable, unimpaired, and constant grace is, the more beautiful is the soul, and the more like to him in whom, as the apostle says, 'There is no instability.' And it is right that the soul should resemble Jesus its spouse in behaviour and in virtues, wholly conformed to him in the stability of perfect love. But this happens seldom, and nowhere except in the true spouse of Christ.

For one who recognizes no variation in his experience of grace, but thinks that it is always at full tide, stable and constant, is either wholly perfect or wholly blind. When a soul is perfect, it is isolated from all carnal affections and from contact with created things. All barriers of corruption and sin between God and the soul are broken down, and he is perfectly united to him in peace and love. But this is an unique grace, transcending human nature. And a man is very blind if he imagines himself to be in a state of grace without feeling God's inspiration, and thinks himself to be established in grace, as though all his feelings and actions were the fruit of special grace; for such a person imagines that everything that he does, feels, and says is inspired by grace, and that this favour will never be withdrawn. If there is such a person—and I hope there is not—he is entirely ignorant of the ways in which grace is experienced.

But you might say that we should love by faith alone, and have no desire for spiritual experiences nor overestimate them if they occur, since the apostle says: *Justus ex fide vivit* (Heb. 10:38). The righteous man lives by faith. I reply that we should not desire physical experiences, however pleasant, nor overestimate them should they occur. But we should always desire spiritual experiences such as I am speaking of now, if they come about in the way that I mentioned earlier. These experiences include the uprooting of all love of the world, the opening of the eyes of the spirit, purity of spirit, peace of conscience, and others similar. We should desire always to be conscious—so far as we may—of the lively inspiration of grace brought about by the spiritual presence of God within our souls. We should desire to contemplate him constantly with reverence, and always to feel the sweetness of his love in the wondrous nearness of his presence. This should be our life, and this our experience of grace, for God is the source of all grace, and grants this gift as he wills, to some in greater measure and to others less. For he grants this experience of his presence in various ways, as he sees best. And this experience is the goal towards which we should direct our lives and exertions, for without it we cannot live the life of the spirit. For just as the soul is the life of the body, God is the life of the soul by his gracious presence. But however real this experience may be, it is as yet only in faith, and cannot be compared to the experience of God himself which we shall enjoy in the bliss of heaven.

We should have a deep desire for this experience, for every rational soul should desire with all its strength to draw close to God, and to be united to him by its awareness of his unseen presence. It is easier to attain knowledge of this presence by personal experience than by reading books, for it is life and love, strength and light, joy and peace to a chosen soul. A soul that has once experienced it cannot therefore lose it without pain; it cannot cease to desire it, because it is so good in itself, and brings such comfort. And what can bring greater comfort to a soul than to be withdrawn by grace from the clamour of worldly affairs, from the corruption of its own desires, and from unprofitable love of creatures into the peace and joy of spiritual love? Nothing can exceed this joy. Nothing can bring greater joy to one who loves God than his own gracious presence revealed to a pure soul. He is never depressed or sad except when he feels imprisoned by the body, and he is never completely glad or happy except when he is utterly unconscious of self, as he is when he contemplates God in the spirit. However, perfect joy is not possible in this life, because the heavy burden of bodily corruption oppresses his soul, bearing it down and greatly lessening his spiritual joy: and this must always be so as long as he remains in this life.

Nevertheless, when I speak of these variations of grace, how it comes and goes, do not fall into the error of thinking that I am referring to the ordinary grace possessed and experienced by a man through faith and goodwill towards God. Unless he possesses and perseveres in this grace, he cannot be saved, for it exists in the least of chosen souls. I am speaking of the special grace that is inspired by the Holy Spirit, as I mentioned earlier. Ordinary grace, that is, charity, remains undiminished whatever a man may do, as long as his will is directed towards God, so that he would not commit mortal sin or do anything that is forbidden as a mortal sin, for this grace is only lost through sin. Sin is mortal when a man's conscience warns him that it is mortal, and yet he deliberately does it. The same applies if a man's conscience is so blinded that he deliberately does something that is forbidden under pain of mortal sin by God and his Church.

The awareness of special grace that accompanies the invisible presence of God and makes the soul perfect in love, does not always continue at its highest intensity, but comes and goes unpredictably as I have said. For our Lord says: *Spiritus ubi vult spirat: et vocem ejus audis, et nescis unde veniat, aut quo vadat* (John 3:8). The Holy Spirit breathes where he wills, and you hear his voice; but you do not know whence he comes or whither he goes. Sometimes he comes secretly when you are least aware of him, but you will recognize him unmistakably before he goes, for he stirs your heart in a wonderful way, and moves it strongly to contemplate his goodness. Then your heart melts with delight at the tenderness of his love like wax before the fire, and this is the sound of his voice. Then before you realize it, he departs. He withdraws a little, but not entirely, and the soul passes from ecstasy into tranquillity. The intense awareness of his presence passes away, but the effects of grace remain as long as the soul keeps itself pure, and does not wilfully lapse into carelessness and worldliness, or take refuge in outward things. For sometimes it will do so out of natural weakness, and not because it has any pleasure in them. It is this variability in grace that I have just been discussing. //

50 ━━━━━━━━━━━━━━━━━━━━━━━━━━━ Chapter 42

A commendation of the prayer offered to God by a contemplative soul: how stability in prayer is a sure foundation; how every experience of grace in a chosen soul may be said to be of God; and the purer the soul the higher the grace received

When man's soul is untouched by special grace, it is sluggish and incapable of spiritual activity, unable to make progress. This is due to its own weakness, because by nature it is cold and dry, lacking devotion or delight in spiritual things. Then it is touched by grace, and becomes quick and refined, ready for and capable of spiritual activity. This liberates it, and makes it eager to respond to and cooperate with every stirring of grace. Sometimes this grace will move the soul to pray, and I will now tell you about this form of prayer.

The prayers that people use most frequently and find most helpful are probably the Our Father and the Psalms; the Our Father for the simple, and psalms, hymns, and other devotions of the Church for the educated. Having received this grace, a person will not use these prayers as he did before, nor in the usual way that people pray, using a loud voice or a normal tone. His prayer will be uttered in a very low voice and with deep feeling, because his mind is not troubled or distracted by outward things, but wholly withdrawn from them, and his soul is as it were in the presence of God. Therefore every word and syllable is uttered with understanding, sweetness, and delight, and his lips and heart are in complete harmony. This is because the soul has been set on fire with love, and all its interior prayer is like a flame leaping from a firebrand, kindling every power of the soul and transforming them into love. It fires them with such consolation that the soul desires to 'pray without ceasing', and to do nothing else. The more the soul prays in this way, the better it is able to pray, and the stronger it becomes. For grace brings great help to the soul, and renders everything light and easy, so that it takes delight in reciting the psalms and sings the praises of God with heavenly joy and sweetness.

This spiritual activity is the food of the soul, and this form of prayer is of great power, for it reduces and defeats all the temptations of the devil, both subtle and open. It removes all memory and love of the world, and of carnal sins. It protects both body and soul from being overwhelmed by the sorrows of this life. It keeps the soul alive to the workings of grace and divine love within it, and constantly feeds the flame of love as sticks feed a fire. It dispels all weariness and dejection, and fills the soul with joy and gladness. Of this prayer David says: *Dirigatur oratio mea sicut incensum in conspectu tuo* (Ps. 141:2). Let my prayer ascend in your sight, O Lord, as the incense. For as incense cast on to the fire causes a fragrant odour as the smoke rises into the air, so a psalm sung or said with love and understanding in a fervent heart rises as a fragrant odour in the sight of God and the whole company of heaven.

No fly tries to rest on the rim of a pot boiling over a fire; similarly, no worldly desire can survive in a pure soul that is enveloped and warmed in the fire of love, boiling over with psalms and praises to God. This is true prayer. It is always heard by God, gives glory to him, and is rewarded by his grace. It makes the soul the friend of God and of all the angels of heaven. Therefore let anyone who can pray in this way do so, for it is good and brings great grace.

Although this form of prayer is not full contemplation, and is not due to the direct action of divine love itself, it is nevertheless a measure of contemplation, for it cannot be practised without abundant grace through the opening of the eyes of the spirit. Therefore one who has attained this freedom and state of grace, and has tasted its heavenly joy, has reached a certain degree of contemplation.

This kind of prayer is a rich offering of devotion, which is taken by the angels and presented before the face of God. The prayer of those who are engaged in active works has a double nature, for while their preoccupation with worldly matters often causes them to have one thing in their minds while the words of the psalm they are reciting expresses another. However, provided that their intention is right, their prayer is good and commendable, although it lacks savour and devotion. But the prayer offered by a contemplative has a single nature, for heart and lips are in complete harmony. The soul is so integrated by grace, and so detached from worldly things, that it is master of the body. The body then becomes no more than an instrument and trumpet of the soul, on which it sweetly sounds the spiritual praises of God.

This is the trumpet of which David speaks: *Buccinate in neomenia tuba, in insigni [die] solemnitatis vestrae* (Ps. 81:3). Sound the trumpet at new moon. Meaning: You souls who have been reformed in the spiritual life by the opening of your spiritual eyes, sing psalms with devotion, and blow on the trumpet of your bodily tongues. This prayer is so pleasing to God and so profitable to the soul, that anyone who is newly turned to God, who wishes to please him, and to receive his special grace, should have a strong desire for it. He should strive by grace to attain this freedom of spirit, so that he may offer his prayers and praises to God constantly, stably, and devoutly, fixing his whole mind and ardent love on him alone, and be ready to pray in this way whenever grace moves him to it.

This is a sure and true form of prayer. If you can practise it and remain steadfast in it, you have no need to go around here and there asking every spiritual man what you should do, how you should love God, how you should serve him, and discussing spiritual matters that are beyond your understanding, as some may do. This is not at all profitable unless it is really necessary. Hold fast to your prayer even if it is difficult at first, so that you may in time reach this peaceful state of spiritual prayer. This will bring you all the knowledge you need, and guard you from all deception and illusion. If you already possess this grace, try to preserve it and do not give it up; but if it is withdrawn from you for a time, and you are moved to pray in another way, then leave it and resume it later. Whoever has the grace of this kind of prayer has no need to ask what he should fix his thought upon during prayer, whether upon the words of a prayer, or upon God, or the name of Jesus, for his experience of this grace is a sure guide. For the eyes of the soul turn to God and contemplate him clearly, and it knows with certainty that it knows and sees him. I do not mean that it sees him as he is in the fullness of his Godhead, but that it sees him to whatever extent he wills to reveal himself to a pure soul in this mortal life, according to the measure of its purity. For you can be sure that every experience of grace is an experience of God himself, and may be called God; and the soul's experience of God is greater or less in proportion to its own degree of grace. Indeed, the soul's first experience of special grace at the beginning of the spiritual life—the grace of compunction and contrition for its sins—is an experience of God himself, since it is he who infuses contrition into a soul by his presence. At that time the soul has only a crude and elementary knowledge of God, and has no experience of the nature of his Godhead, for its own impurity prevents it seeing him clearly. But later, if it grows in virtue and purity, grace will bring it to a fuller vision and experience of God. This experience will be of a more spiritual nature, and correspond more nearly to the nature of God himself.

What is most pleasing to God is to have a soul become by grace what he is by nature, and this is achieved through spiritual contemplation and love of him. And this must be the aim of all who love God. So whenever you feel your soul moved by grace, especially in the way I have described, by the opening of your spiritual eyes, you may be sure that you are seeing and experiencing God. Hold fast to him, try to retain this grace, and do not easily let him go. Seek God alone for himself, and cooperate with his grace with increased devotion, so that it may grow within you more and more. And although your experience of God is not of him as he is in the fullness of his Godhead, have no fear that you may be deceived if you surrender to your feeling. If you truly love God, be sure that your experience is real, and that by his grace you may have as true an experience and vision of him as is possible in this life. Therefore surrender yourself to this experience when grace draws you, and maintain it with love and delight, in order that you may gradually reach a fuller and better knowledge of God. For grace itself will always direct you if you yield to its guidance until you reach your end.

You may possibly wonder why I say at one time that grace does all this, and at another that it is divine love, or Jesus, or God. My reply is that when I say that grace does it I mean both divine love, Jesus, and God; for all are one and inseparable. Jesus is divine love, Jesus is grace, and Jesus is God, for he does everything within us by grace through his divine love as God. So when writing of this matter I may use whichever of these names I please.

How a soul, by the opening of its spiritual eyes, receives the grace of love, which enables it to understand holy scripture; and how God, hidden in the scriptures, reveals himself to those who love him

When one who loves God has this experience of God in prayer as I have described, he thinks that he will always retain it. But it sometimes happens that grace puts an end to vocal prayer, and calls on the soul to see and experience God in a different way. At first it moves the soul to see God in holy scripture, where God, who is truth, is hidden under the precious cloak of beautiful language, for he wills to be seen and known only by the pure in heart. For truth will not reveal itself to those who hate it, but only to friends who love and seek it with a humble heart. For truth and humility are true sisters, united in love and charity, and there is no disharmony between them. Humility depends on truth, and not on itself, while truth depends on humility, so that they are in complete accord. Insofar, therefore, as the soul of one who loves God is made humble by the opening of its spiritual eyes through grace, recognizing its own nothingness, trusting entirely in the mercy and goodness of God, and depending solely on his help and favour, it has a true desire for him, and so sees him. For it sees the truths of holy scripture clearly and marvellously revealed in a manner far beyond the reach of arduous study or natural intelligence. And this may well be termed an experience or perception of God, since God is the well of wisdom, and by infusing a small portion of his wisdom into a pure soul, he enables it to understand all holy scripture. This wisdom is not bestowed on a soul all at once in a single revelation but through grace it receives a new and lasting ability to understand anything that comes to its notice.

This clear understanding is brought about by the presence of God within the soul. For in the Gospel we are told how two disciples were going to Emmaus, burning with love for Jesus and speaking of him, when he appeared to them in the guise of a pilgrim, and taught them how the prophecies of scripture applied to himself. *Aperuit illis sensum, ut intelligerent Scripturas* (Luke 24:45). He opened their minds to understand the meaning of the scriptures. In the same way the spiritual presence of Jesus opens the minds of those who love him and burn with desire for him. Through the ministry of the angels it brings the words and teachings of holy scripture to their minds without effort and study, and reveals their meaning, however difficult or obscure. Indeed, the more difficult and remote from human understanding they are, the greater the joy of the soul when their true meaning is revealed to it by God himself. And if the words permit it, they are interpreted both in a literal, moral, mystical, and heavenly sense. By the literal interpretation, which is the simplest and most direct, man's natural intelligence is satisfied. By the moral interpretation of scripture the soul is taught about virtues and vices, and enabled to distinguish between them. By the mystical interpretation the soul is illumined to recognize God's workings within his Church, and to apply the words of scripture to Christ our head, and to his mystical body, the Church. The fourth, or heavenly, interpretation refers solely to the activity of love, and attributes all the truths of scripture to the workings of love. And since this corresponds most closely to the experience of heaven, I call it heavenly.

One who loves God is his friend, not because he has deserved this privilege, but because God in his merciful goodness takes him as his friend with a solemn pledge. He reveals his secrets to him, and treats him as a true friend who pleases and loves him, and does not merely serve him with fear like a slave. Thus Jesus himself says to his apostles: *Iam vos dixi amicos, quia quaecumque audivi a Patre meo, nota feci vobis* (John 15:15). I now call you my friends, for I make known to you all that I have heard from my Father. To a pure soul, whose palate is cleansed from the corruption of worldly love, holy scripture is nourishing food and delicious sustenance. Its taste is wonderfully sweet when fully assimilated by the understanding, for within it is concealed the life-giving spirit which quickens all the powers of the soul, and fills them with heavenly sweetness and spiritual delight. But anyone who wishes to eat this spiritual bread must have good teeth, white and clean, for heretics and those who love the world cannot pierce its inmost substance. Their teeth are dirty, so that they cannot taste its true savour. By teeth we mean the interior powers of the soul, which in lovers of the world and heretics are rotten with sin and vanity. They would like to reach the true knowledge of holy scripture by the exercise of their own reason, but they cannot do so, for their reason is corrupted both by original and actual sin, and is not yet healed by grace. As a result they can only gnaw on the outer bark, and whatever they may say to the contrary, they are incapable of reaching the inner savour. They are not humble and pure enough to find it, nor are they the friends of God, so that he does not reveal his secrets to them.

The secrets of holy scripture are locked away and sealed with the signet of God's finger, which is the Holy Spirit, so that none may learn them without his love and grace. God alone holds the key of knowledge, as scripture says, and he himself is the key. He admits whom he will by the inspiration of his grace, and does not break the seal. And this is how God treats those who love him. He does not treat all in the same way, but grants special favours to those who are inspired to seek truth in the scriptures after devout prayer and diligent study. These may learn the truths of God when he chooses to reveal them.

See, then, how grace opens the eyes of the soul and enlightens its understanding in a wonderful manner beyond the capabilities of our weak and fallen nature. As I said earlier, it gives the soul a new ability to understand holy scripture and to grasp its truths, whether it is reading it or meditating upon it. It is enabled to understand the spiritual meaning of all the words and teachings that it hears. And this is nothing strange, for the spirit that reveals its meaning for the comfort of a pure soul is the Holy Spirit who first inspired it. This grace is granted to the unlettered as well as to the learned, for these can and do grasp the substance, the truth and the spiritual savour of holy scripture. And although they may not understand all its implications, this is not necessary for them. And when grace gives the soul this ability and enlightenment, it sometimes wishes to be alone, away from the distraction of creatures, in order to employ freely the instrument of reason, and consider the truths contained in holy scripture. At such times sufficient words, teachings, and phrases will come to mind, and keep the soul regularly and profitably occupied.

A soul can only learn by experience what comfort and spiritual joy, savour, and sweetness this light of grace may bring to it, whether inward perceptions, hidden knowledge, and sudden visitations of the Holy Spirit. And I am sure that such a soul will not go astray provided that its teeth—that is, its spiritual senses—are kept white and clean from pride and intellectual presumption. I think that David was experiencing great joy in this way when he said: *Quam dulcia faucibus meis eloquia tua, super mel ori meo* (Ps. 119:103). How sweet are your words to my lips, O Lord; sweeter than honey to my mouth. That is: O Lord God, your holy words, recorded in holy scripture and brought to my mind by grace, are sweeter to my lips—that is, to the affections of my soul—than honey to my mouth. How wonderful it is to see God in this way without wearisome labour!

As I said earlier, this is one way of seeing God. We do not see him as he is, but under the forms of works and words, *per speculum etiam in aenigmate:* in a glass and under a symbol, as the apostle says (I Cor. 13:12). God is infinite power, wisdom and goodness, righteousness, truth, holiness, and mercy. But what God is in himself none may see or know, but he may be seen in his works by the light of grace. His power is seen in his creation of all things out of nothing, his wisdom in his ordered disposition of them, his holiness in his gifts of grace, his righteousness in the punishment of sin, his truth in his sure reward of good works. All these things are shown in holy scripture, where the soul sees them together with all the other attributes of God. Hence you may see how such knowledge, whether bestowed through the holy scriptures or through any other writings inspired by grace, is nothing other than an affectionate correspondence between a loving soul and Jesus whom it loves: or more correctly, between Jesus the true lover and the souls whom he loves. He has a tender love for all his chosen children who are subject to the limitations of this mortal body, and therefore although he dwells apart from them, hidden from their sight in the bosom of the Father and in full enjoyment of the Godhead, yet he bears them in his heart, and often visits them with his presence and his grace. He comforts them with his words in holy scripture, and drives away heaviness and weariness, doubts and fears from their hearts. He gives gladness and joy to all who truly believe his promises, and humbly abide the fulfilment of his will.

St Paul said: *Quaecumque scripta sunt, ad nostram doctrinam scripta sunt, ut per consolationem Scripturarum spem habeamus* (Rom. 15:4). All that is written for our learning is written that through the consolation of the scriptures we may have hope of salvation. And this is another aspect of contemplation, that once our spiritual eyes are opened, we see God in the scriptures. The clearer our vision in contemplation, the deeper the love of God that we feel. When a pure soul experiences even a little of this grace given through the scriptures, it will set little value on the seven sciences or on any worldly knowledge.

For the end of this sacred knowledge is the salvation of the soul in eternal life, while unless grace re-directs it to this right end, the end of the other is but vanity and passing satisfaction.

52 ———————————————————— Chapter 44

How the secret voice of God sounds within the soul, and how the illuminations brought to the soul by grace may be called God's voice

These new experiences within a pure soul are wonderful, and could a soul enjoy them continually, it might truthfully be described as partly reformed in feeling, although not as yet fully. For God reveals even more to it, and draws it closer to himself. He begins to speak to it even more intimately and lovingly, and the soul is eager to respond to the stirrings of grace. For the prophet says: *Quocumque ibat spiritus, illuc gradiebantur et rotae sequentes eum* (Ezek. 1:20). Wherever the spirit goes, there go the wheels following him. The wheels represent the true lovers of God, because they are perfectly round in virtue, without any angle of obstinacy, and they turn freely because their wills conform to the movements of grace. For, as the prophet says, they obey and act as grace moves and directs them. But before they do so, they are able to make a sure test and verification of this voice of grace, so that they are not deceived by their own imagination or by the devil. Our Lord says of those that love him: *Oves meae vocem mean audiunt, et cognosco eas, et cognoscunt me meae* (John 10:27). My sheep hear my voice, and I know them, and they know me. The secret voice of God is true, and it makes the soul true. In it there is no deception or illusion, no pride or hypocrisy, but gentleness, humility, peace, love, and charity, and it is full of life and grace. So when this voice sounds within a soul, it is sometimes so powerful that the soul immediately lays aside whatever it is doing—whether prayer, speaking, reading, meditation, or any physical occupation—and listens to it alone. And as it listens to the sweet sound of God's voice, it is filled with peace and love, transported far beyond all thought of earthly things. In this peace God reveals himself to the soul, sometimes as Lord to be feared, sometimes as a Father to be reverenced, and sometimes as a spouse to be loved.

At such times the soul is absorbed in a wonderful reverence and loving contemplation of God, which brings it a delight far transcending anything it has ever known. It enjoys so great a sense of security and peace in God, and so acute a realization of his goodness, that it wishes always to remain in this state, and never to do anything else. The soul feels that it is touching God himself, and by virtue of his ineffable touch it is made whole and stable, reverently contemplating God alone, as though nothing existed save God and itself. At these times it is upheld solely by his favour and wonderful goodness, and is profoundly conscious of this truth.

This feeling often comes without any special study of holy scripture, and with only a few words in mind. But the soul may employ words to give expression to the feelings in its heart, whether of love or worship. While it enjoys this grace, it is far removed from all love of the world, and from any thought of it: it pays no attention to it, and has no time to spare for it. At these times grace will bring to the soul certain illuminations, which I call the words of God and the perception of spiritual things. For you will realize that the whole purpose of God's action in a soul is to make it his true and perfect spouse in the height and fullness of love. And because this cannot be done suddenly, God who is love, and wisest of all lovers, employs many wonderful ways to bring this about. And in order that the chosen soul may come to be truly united to himself, he addresses it in the gracious words of a lover. He shows it his wonders, and gives it rich gifts, promising even more, and showing it great affection and courtesy. I cannot describe the workings of God in detail, nor is it necessary. Nevertheless I will say something as grace inspires me.

Firstly, when the eyes of a pure soul have been opened, it is drawn towards perfect love by the revelation of spiritual matters, not in order that the soul should rest content with these and cease its quest, but that it should seek and love God himself, who is above all things, having no regard for anything but him. If you enquire about the nature of these spiritual matters that I am often speaking of, my answer is that they are all the truths revealed in holy scripture. Therefore a soul that by the light of grace comprehends the truths of the scriptures sees these spiritual things to which I have referred.

Chapter 45

How when grace opens the eyes of a soul, it is given wisdom which enables it humbly and surely to recognize the various degrees in the Church Militant, and the nature of the angels

Nevertheless, there are other spiritual matters that the light of grace reveals to the soul, and they are these. The nature of rational souls, and how God works in them by grace: the nature and activity of the angels, both blessed and fallen: and the knowledge of the Blessed Trinity in so far as grace reveals it.

Scripture says of the spouse in the Song of Songs: *Surgam et circuibo civitatem: et quaeram quem diligit anima mea* (S. of S. 3:2). I shall rise and go about the city, and seek him whom my soul loves. That is, I shall lift up my thoughts and go about the city. This city symbolizes the whole of creation, both material and spiritual, which by God's decree is governed by the laws of nature, of reason, and of grace. I go about this city when I study the nature and origins of material creatures, the gifts of grace, and the joy of spiritual beings. And in all these I seek him whom my soul loves. It is wonderful for the eyes of the soul to see God in the material universe, and to see his power, his wisdom, and his goodness in the ordering of it [. . .]

How by the same light the soul may perceive the nature of the blessed angels, and recognize how Jesus is both God and man, transcending all things

And after this by the same light the soul may see the beauty of the angels, the nobility of their nature, the refinement of their being, and

how they are confirmed in grace and in the fulness of eternal bliss
[. . .]

But with the help of the angels the soul sees even more. For a pure
soul rises above all these things to contemplate the blessed nature of
Jesus himself. First it sees his glorious manhood, and that it is rightly
exalted above the nature of all angels. Then it begins to contemplate
his divinity, for knowledge of creatures leads a soul to knowledge of
the creator. The soul then begins to perceive a little of the mysteries
of the Blessed Trinity. And it may well do this, for the light of grace
is its guide, and it will not err so long as it walks in this light.

Then, so far as it is possible in this life, the soul clearly perceives
the unity of substance and the distinction of persons in the Blessed
Trinity, and it understands many other truths concerning the Trinity
which are set forth and interpreted by the doctors of the Church in
their writings. And these selfsame truths concerning the Blessed
Trinity which the holy doctors are inspired to set forth in their books
for our instruction may be perceived by a pure soul by the light of
grace. But I will not enlarge on this matter, for it is not necessary.

When enabled to do so by special grace, the soul feels wonderful
love and heavenly joy in the contemplation of this truth, for light and
love are inseparable in a pure soul. For no love that springs from
contemplation brings the soul so close to God as this does; it is the
highest and most perfect knowledge of Jesus, God and man, that the
light of grace can bring to a soul. Therefore the burning love kindled
by this is greater than that kindled by any knowledge of created things,
whether material or spiritual.

All this knowledge of God's creation and of God himself, the
creator and sustainer of the entire universe, which is infused into a
soul by grace as I have mentioned, I call the fair words and communi-
cations of God to the soul chosen as his true spouse. He reveals mysteries and often offers rich gifts to it out of his treasury, and adorns the
soul with them with great honour. She has no need to be ashamed
when she appears before the face of God her spouse in the company
of her fellows. All this loving and intimate conversation between God
and the soul may be called a secret word, of which holy scripture says:
*Porro ad me dictum est verbum absconditum, et venas susurri ejus percepit
auris mea* (Job 4:12). A secret word is spoken to me, and my ear has
caught the low murmur of his voice. The inspiration of God is a
secret word, for it is hidden from all who love the world, and revealed
to those who love him. It is by this means that a pure soul readily

catches the sound of his murmured words, by which he reveals his truth. For each truth revealed by grace, and received with inward delight and joy, is a secret murmur of God in the ear of a pure soul.

One who wishes to hear these sweet spiritual murmurs of God must possess great purity of soul, meekness, and all other virtues, and be partly deaf to the clamour of the world. This is the voice of God, of which David said: *Vox Domini praeparantis cervos, et revelabit condensa* (Ps. 29:9). The voice of God prepares the harts, and he will show them the thickets. That is: the inspiration of God makes souls as light as harts, that spring up from the ground and leap over the bushes and briars of worldly vanity. And he shows them the thickets, that is, his secrets, which can be discerned only by sharp eyes. This contemplation, surely founded in grace and humility, makes a soul wise, and fires it with a longing to see the face of God. These are the spiritual matters that I spoke of earlier, and they may be called new experiences of grace. I only touch on them briefly, for the guidance of your soul. For a soul that is pure, and moved by grace to engage in this spiritual activity of contemplation, may learn more in an hour than could be written in a long book.

LAUS DEO